What

ST EM

Can Do
for Your Classroom

Improving Student Problem Solving,
Collaboration, and Engagement

GRADES K-6

Jason
McKenna

Solution Tree | Press

a division of
Solution Tree

555 North Morton Street
Bloomington, IN 47404
800.733.6786 (toll free) / 812.336.7700
FAX: 812.336.7790

email: info@SolutionTree.com
SolutionTree.com

Visit **go.SolutionTree.com/instruction** to download the free reproducibles in this book.

Printed in the United States of America

Library of Congress Cataloging-in-Publication Data

Names: McKenna, Jason, author.
Title: What STEM can do for your classroom : improving student problem
  solving, collaboration, and engagement, Grades K-6 / Jason McKenna.
Other titles: What Science, Technology, Engineering, Mathematics can do for
  your classroom
Description: Bloomington, IN : Solution Tree Press, [2023] | Includes
  bibliographical references and index.
Identifiers: LCCN 2022033753 (print) | LCCN 2022033754 (ebook) | ISBN
  9781954631458 (Paperback) | ISBN 9781954631465 (eBook)
Subjects: LCSH: Science--Study and teaching (Elementary)--United States. |
  Technology--Study and teaching (Elementary)--United States. |
  Engineering--Study and teaching (Elementary)--United States. |
  Mathematics--Study and teaching (Elementary)--United States. |
  Technological literacy--United States.
Classification: LCC LB1585.3 .M45 2023 (print) | LCC LB1585.3 (ebook) |
  DDC 372.35--dc23/eng/20221125
LC record available at https://lccn.loc.gov/2022033753
LC ebook record available at https://lccn.loc.gov/2022033754

Solution Tree
Jeffrey C. Jones, CEO
Edmund M. Ackerman, President

Solution Tree Press
President and Publisher: Douglas M. Rife
Associate Publisher: Sarah Payne-Mills
Managing Production Editor: Kendra Slayton
Editorial Director: Todd Brakke
Art Director: Rian Anderson
Copy Chief: Jessi Finn
Senior Production Editor: Sarah Foster
Content Development Specialist: Amy Rubenstein
Copy Editor: Jessi Finn
Proofreader: Madonna Evans
Text and Cover Designer: Kelsey Hoover
Associate Editor: Sarah Ludwig
Editorial Assistants: Charlotte Jones and Elijah Oates

To my daughter, Josephine, who taught me everything.

ACKNOWLEDGMENTS

Solution Tree Press would like to thank the following reviewers:

Kim Buckley
Second-Grade Teacher
Katonah Elementary School
Katonah, New York

Jennifer Evans
Principal
Burnham School
Cicero, Illinois

Janet Gilbert
Principal
Mountain Shadows Elementary School
Glendale, Arizona

Erin Kruckenberg
Fifth-Grade Teacher
Jefferson Elementary School
Harvard, Illinois

Karen Matteson
District Instructional Coach
  & Math Specialist
Cortland Enlarged City School District
Cortland, New York

Ashley Richey
Mathematics Instructional Coach
East Pointe Elementary School
Greenwood, Arkansas

Lauren Smith
Instructional Coach
Noble Crossing Elementary School,
  Noblesville Schools
Noblesville, Indiana

Rea Smith
Math Facilitator
Rogers Public Schools
Rogers, Arkansas

Lori Wilds
Principal
California Elementary School
West Covina, California

Visit **go.SolutionTree.com/instruction** to download the free reproducibles in this book.

TABLE OF CONTENTS

PART THREE: Explore STEM Pedagogy **71**

CHAPTER 5

Exploring STEM Teaching and Guided Discovery Learning **73**

CHAPTER 6

Making Assessment Student Centered in Elementary STEM Classrooms **91**

CHAPTER 7

Exploring STEM and Creativity

CHAPTER 8

Bringing It All Together

ABOUT THE AUTHOR

 **Jason McKenna** is the director of global educational strategy for VEX Robotics, overseeing all curriculum development and classroom integration for the VEX IQ, VEX GO, VEX 123, VEXcode VR, VEX V5/EXP, and VEX Workcell platforms. An educational strategist with twenty years of experience teaching in elementary classrooms, McKenna ensures VEX Robotics' educational STEM solutions align with global educational standards and fulfill educators' needs.

To keep his finger on the pulse of society's needs, McKenna travels the world to meet with parents, educators, and key government stakeholders and discuss the challenges of preparing students for a 21st century, knowledge-based economy. He develops and implements research-based STEM education solutions that use differentiated instruction and assessment to further student learning.

Many of McKenna's articles have been published. In addition, he collaborated with the Carnegie Mellon Robotics Academy on STEM education research funded by the National Science Foundation and the U.S. Defense Advanced Research Projects Agency to improve how teachers teach STEM in U.S. schools.

McKenna holds a master of education in curriculum and instruction from California University of Pennsylvania (now PennWest California). He received his undergraduate degree in elementary education from Geneva College. He is also a Carnegie Mellon Robotics Academy Certified Master Instructor.

To learn more about McKenna's work, visit https://jmckenna.org or follow @mckennaj72 on Twitter.

To book Jason McKenna for professional development, contact pd@Solution Tree.com.

Introduction

Thousands of excited grade 4 through college students filled Freedom Hall in Louisville, Kentucky, for the unveiling of the 2019–2020 VEX Robotics Competition. The massive energy in the arena made it feel like a rock concert. As I walked out of the arena with Bob Mimlitch, cofounder of VEX Robotics, he said, "What is ironic is how excited these students are for the hundreds of hours of work they are about to begin" (B. Mimlitch, personal communication, April 27, 2019). His comment floored me. He was right. Their eagerness to engage in hundreds of hours of science, technology, engineering, and mathematics (STEM)—often after school and on weekends—was a teacher's dream.

This book's goal is to help you create that same eagerness and energy while teaching STEM in your classroom. I begin here with a quick summary of how I started in STEM and a breakdown of who this book is for and what's in it.

How I Started With STEM

Teaching STEM changed my life. It began when my fifth- and sixth-grade students dragged me into STEM because they wanted to learn how to build and program robots, even though I don't have a background in engineering or coding. When I started teaching STEM and robotics, I was maybe only a day (or a few minutes) ahead of my students. Despite that, I realized that concepts I had struggled to teach for years became easier when I started teaching STEM. For example, through their STEM learning, my elementary students learned to more effectively explore multiple ways to solve problems, build their understanding that first answers may not be correct, and work collaboratively on projects.

Now, as the director of educational strategy at VEX Robotics, I've been fortunate to see hundreds of classrooms engage their students to learn the same concepts. Government leaders have told me that STEM in their schools helps transform their countries' economies from service based to knowledge based. In addition, teachers have told me how rewarding it is to see their students plan to become engineers one day. For me, it's highly rewarding to see nervous and reluctant teachers who thought that they could never teach STEM incorporate STEM into their classrooms and schools successfully. Teachers are amazing when given the right tools, training, and support. This book uses examples from my experience of teaching robotics to help teachers be amazing. The reason why so many of the examples in the book are from robotics is that I have found robotics to be the best organizer for STEM lessons and activities. This doesn't mean that you need to begin teaching robotics, but you can see integrated STEM in action and use those examples to inspire your own activities and lessons.

Who Should Read This Book

Although I refer specifically to elementary teachers throughout, this book is for all K–6 teachers who need practical, research-based strategies and methods to implement STEM in their classrooms. Because I believe all teachers can benefit from teaching STEM, I provide information and context so you can make informed decisions about implementing STEM. Some teachers may teach STEM all the time (as I did), or some may use STEM to make mathematics classes more hands-on and engaging. Your implementation is just that—yours.

I also hope more experienced STEM teachers will use this book to enhance what they are already doing with STEM. In addition, elementary administrators and instructional leaders can use this book to discover ways to implement STEM and support teachers as they begin or expand their journey into STEM teaching.

What Is in This Book

Many books, TED Talks, presentations, and more discuss teaching STEM. However, this book differs from many because it doesn't align with the following claims.

- Schools are killing creativity.

- Teaching STEM requires a new way of teaching.

- Schools should de-emphasize teaching knowledge and instead focus on teaching knowledge strategies.

Good STEM teaching is good teaching. If you are a great mathematics or reading teacher, you will probably be a great STEM teacher. To help you succeed in the classroom, this book provides the context of STEM education and its practical classroom applications. Each chapter features research, information, and educator conversations about STEM education. These educators include classroom teachers, authors, and scientists. Each chapter also features materials you can use to improve your classroom and teaching. Finally, this book's three parts and eight chapters focus on the *why* and *how* of STEM education.

Part 1: Start STEM Early

Chapter 1 discusses what STEM is and the importance of teaching STEM. This chapter contains rich examples of how STEM is a mirror of our world and how the teaching of STEM connects students to their world. Chapter 2 discusses the importance of STEM in the early grades. Elementary students are natural scientists and engineers. They look to experiment, play, question, and discover. However, young students also begin forming opinions about their proficiency in STEM. Therefore, we teachers must reach these students before they decide they aren't good at mathematics (or science or engineering, and so on). These chapters provide techniques to combat negative perceptions of their abilities and begin incorporating STEM in the classroom.

Part 2: Discover STEM Learning Principles

Chapter 3 focuses on creating classrooms full of highly engaged students and fostering student ownership and choice. Chapter 4 discusses the learning principles of STEM (the context for STEM pedagogy). In addition, these chapters explore how to keep students motivated and engaged during STEM lessons while also exploring how to build resilience and risk taking with our elementary students.

Part 3: Explore STEM Pedagogy

Chapter 5 explores the concept of *guided discovery*, which blends direct instruction and open-ended inquiry from students. A big part of guided discovery is the proper scaffolding of lessons, and this chapter details how to do that scaffolding.

Chapter 6 covers assessment. When I started teaching STEM, I struggled with what I should do for formative assessment while the students worked collaboratively on their STEM projects. STEM pedagogy is often described as student centered, but what about assessment? How do we make assessment student centered too?

Chapter 7 details how to teach creativity. Teaching students to be more creative is a common goal, but the details often end there. "What is creativity? How can I identify it in my classroom? How do I foster creativity?" Chapter 7 answers all those questions and more.

Finally, chapter 8 pulls everything together and provides examples of STEM implementation. In addition, chapter 8 includes teaching vignettes for every grade level, K–6, that highlight techniques and concepts from the book.

Part 1

Start

STEM

Early

When discussing the importance of STEM, many point to the need for more engineers and coders to help fill the jobs of today and tomorrow. Workforce development is important, but STEM is more than an apprenticeship program. Part 1 explores what STEM is and why it is important to expose young students to STEM education.

CHAPTER 1

Inspiring Students With STEM Narratives

STEM is about how we exist.

—Anthony G. Robbins

While Stéphane Bancel, CEO of Moderna, vacationed in France in January 2020, he read about a lung disease spreading in southern China. On his return to the United States, he told the Moderna leadership team that a COVID-19 vaccine was their highest priority (Zuckerman, 2021). At the same time, at BioNTech, cofounders Uğur Şahin and Özlem Türeci worked on their COVID-19 vaccine (Zuckerman, 2021). Less than a year later, hospital workers around the United States received the first shots of the Moderna and Pfizer (U.S. partner of BioNTech) vaccines (Guarino, Cha, Wood, & Witte, 2020).

The creation of COVID-19 vaccines is an incredible scientific achievement; historically, developing and testing a vaccine takes years. So, what made the difference with the COVID-19 vaccines? The development of messenger RNA vaccines, previous work on related viruses, and faster manufacturing methods paved the way for the speedy development of the COVID-19 vaccines (Ball, 2020). In essence, the deep integration of STEM in all aspects of vaccine development made the achievement possible.

Real-world applications often require knowledge across all the STEM disciplines. Similarly, integrated STEM in the classroom helps students build knowledge in individual disciplines and make connections among them (National Academy of Engineering & National Research Council, 2014). Nevertheless, even this view of STEM is limiting. STEM is more than a problem-solving practice—more than an acronym, a method, a job skill, or a lesson plan. This chapter explores science and engineering, giving examples of how they work together, and it explains how teachers can inspire students to embrace STEM. It provides four narratives of real-world STEM projects to inspire teachers and students. Finally, the chapter gives teachers ideas of what to do now in their classrooms and some key takeaways.

Exploring Science and Engineering

When people think of STEM in the real world, they often think of science and engineering, but the processes and purposes underpinning the two disciplines are different. Scientists often begin by trying to understand an individual phenomenon, like the coronavirus that appeared in Wuhan, China, in late 2019 (LaFee, 2021). Therefore, scientific understanding creates a general set of rules (a vaccine) to deal with the phenomenon (coronavirus). Put more simply, scientists focus on a question. They create a hypothesis around a question and then test it using the scientific method.

Engineering often begins with a different perspective, one focused on a product. Engineers tackle a generalized situation (getting from point A to point B quickly and comfortably) and then create specific solutions. Engineering solutions are tailored to individual wants and needs (for example, designing a truck versus a sedan). Therefore, the engineering design process requires iterations and trade-offs because of constraints involved in a specific output. This process consists of three steps: (1) define the problem by identifying situations that people want to change, (2) develop solutions by conveying possible solutions through visual or physical representations, and (3) optimize by comparing, testing, and evaluating solutions. Chapter 4 (page 55) discusses the engineering design process in more detail.

What scientists and engineers have in common are the interest, curiosity, and desire to know more to propel the scientific method and the engineering design process forward. Therefore, scientists and engineers are motivated to investigate and create, which is how they integrate as crucial parts of STEM. As we explore further in chapter 3 (page 37), motivation leads to student engagement, which leads to student learning. Consider the following example of science and engineering working together.

In the 1950s, scientists debated two competing theories about the origins of the universe. The steady-state theory states that the universe has no beginning or end, while the big bang theory states that the universe began nearly fourteen billion years ago (Livio, 2013). Then, in 1964, Bell Labs researchers detected a hiss in a radio antenna that shifted many scientists' opinions to the big bang theory.

The hiss is the *cosmic microwave background*, which showed scientists that the near-perfect uniformity of the microwaves coming from all over the universe meant that the universe was smooth in its infancy. However, the universe we see now is not smooth because matter gathered in clumps over time. Therefore, one of the first challenges of understanding the universe is to determine how it went from smooth to lumpy (Wolchover, 2021).

To answer this question and more, the James Webb Space Telescope launched in 2021. Space telescopes gather light that emanates from objects in space and reflect it toward a mirror (Wolchover, 2021). The mirror then focuses the light on scientific instruments. This captured light has traveled for billions of years across the universe.

The mirror in the James Webb Space Telescope is as big as a house (Wolchover, 2021). Therefore, it is segmented into eighteen hexagonal pieces and folded up for launch. Because the mirror also must be perfectly smooth, the segments must be in virtually perfect alignment. In July 2022, NASA released the first spectacular images from the telescope (NASA, 2022). These images are vital because they contain information about how the earliest galaxies were formed and what was used to form them.

The telescope's combination of science, technology, engineering, and mathematics to answer a crucial question shows the essence of STEM. To begin this process, scientists had to wonder about how the universe began. Then, they formed hypotheses and tested them. This takes a long time. Just the work on the James Webb Space Telescope spanned over twenty years (Wolchover, 2021).

STEM is a mirror that reflects our world and its complexity. Therefore, we need to teach students they can wonder, form hypotheses, and test them to empower students to answer their questions about the world. And this can happen as early as kindergarten.

Seeing Integrated STEM in Action

K–6 students are excellent at wondering about their world, and they want their questions answered. Therefore, we need to find suitable ways to teach about the complexity of our world and its systems by finding the best approaches to teaching STEM. As we saw in the preceding section, the universe is an extraordinarily complex system. However, so is a human cell.

When teaching the phases of mitosis, teachers often assign students to draw a cell's shape and the structures inside it. However, this image of the cell is wrong. For example, mitochondria regularly change shape (Kwon, 2019). They can combine and elongate and split and get smaller. Furthermore, cell membranes are highly complex systems made of complex lipids, each with its own structure, characteristics, and function. Understanding what a cell looks like on the inside is difficult because of its complexity (Pavlus, 2019). However, it is this complexity found inside and around us that drives us to wonder about the universe or how our bodies work.

Teaching students to embrace complexity is fertile ground for learning; unfortunately, some teachers are reluctant to implement integrated STEM for that very same reason. They don't always share in the students' excitement about complexity.

Another challenge is that STEM is often presented to students mainly as a means to ensure future employment. In his book *Learner-Centered Design of Computing Education: Research on Computing for Everyone*, Mark Guzdial (2016) writes that many beliefs and influences impact a student's point of view. Students wonder if learning STEM fits how they view themselves or if people who look and act like them succeed in STEM. If students cannot picture themselves succeeding in STEM or if they think STEM is too difficult to learn, they will not be interested in STEM.

By encouraging students to be curious, to see failure as an opportunity, and to not be afraid to make mistakes, teachers can help sustain their students' sense of wonder about the world. And, in helping them, teachers can reignite their own sense of wonder.

STEM education helps students connect what they learn at school with what is happening in the world around them. From lifesaving vaccines to pictures of black holes, the achievements of STEM have never been more essential, nor have they ever been more prevalent in our lives. Teachers can share the following stories of STEM trailblazers to help inspire students with what they can accomplish with STEM. Sharing the stories of a diverse group of STEM trailblazers gives students a chance to see people who look just like them succeed in STEM careers. Finally, sharing these stories with students helps them understand the rewards of a STEM career.

Searching for Life on Mars

NASA's Mars 2020 mission addresses high-priority science for Mars exploration: life, climate, geology, and humans. The one-ton, six-wheel *Perseverance* rover landed on Mars in February 2021, and it is gathering data on Mars's surface to help inform research on the Red Planet (NASA, n.d.). *Perseverance* houses a small helicopter drone named *Ingenuity* that explores the surroundings of *Perseverance*, helping scientists to drive and navigate its movements. In addition, *Ingenuity* is testing the validity of aerial exploration on Mars because the atmosphere of Mars is just 1 percent as dense as the atmosphere of Earth at sea level (Wall, 2015).

Perseverance's landing site is the Jezero Crater, located just north of Mars's equator. Scientists think the crater was the site of a large lake and river delta around 3.5 billion years ago. On Earth, lakes and river deltas are sources of carbon-containing organic compounds that are the building blocks of life (Wall, 2015). If there were life on Mars, scientists hope to find clues in the Jezero Crater.

The *Perseverance* rover focuses on finding compelling rocks that may contain preserved chemical traces of ancient life or may have been altered by an environment that supported microbial life. After identifying compelling rocks, *Perseverance* drills out a sample, places it in a sealed tube, and caches the samples in one location on the surface. Future missions will retrieve these samples and return them to scientists on Earth.

Table 1.1 shows how NASA's Mars 2020 mission integrates all aspects of STEM.

TABLE 1.1: Examples of Integrated STEM in NASA's Mars 2020 Mission

Science	Technology	Engineering	Mathematics
Perseverance is being used to investigate past signs of microbial life. Scientists are determining how astronauts on future missions could produce oxygen from carbon dioxide in Mars's atmosphere.	Scientists need to understand the impact of Mars's environment on the *Perseverance* rover's instruments. To accomplish this, virtual simulations were created to test how heat and cold impact the instruments.	*Perseverance* was engineered to move, collect samples, collect information from its instruments, and so on. NASA engineers needed to engineer ways to deploy and land *Perseverance* on Mars.	Mathematics determines the exact position of the rover while it travels on Mars. Mathematics also keeps track of *Perseverance*'s position in space at any given time.

Discovering a Key to the COVID-19 Vaccine

The first step in creating a COVID-19 vaccine was understanding the shape and structure of the coronavirus spike protein, not an easy task because of the incredibly complex structures of proteins. In January 2020, infectious disease expert Zhang Yongzhen in Shanghai received samples from the lungs of seven patients from Wuhan (Zuckerman, 2021). Zhang and his team worked for the next forty hours to map the virus's genetic instructions. On Friday, January 10, they sent the genetic sequence to the Virological website (https://virological.org), and scientists around the world began their study (Zuckerman, 2021). Zhang and his team accomplished this feat so quickly because of then-recent technological advances in gene sequencing.

Once scientists had access to the genome, they needed to map it. Leading the effort was a team of researchers from the University of Texas at Austin and the National Institutes of Health. The team had designed and produced samples of its stabilized spike protein mere weeks after receiving the genome sequence of the virus (Kramer, 2020). The speed and accuracy of the researchers were partially due to state-of-the-art technology known as *cryogenic electron microscopy* (cryo-EM). Cryo-EM allows researchers to make atomic-scale 3-D models of cellular structures, molecules, and viruses.

As important as cryo-EM is, scientists use artificial intelligence (AI) to go even further. A team led by Rommie Amaro, professor and endowed chair of chemistry and biochemistry at the University of California San Diego, and Arvind Ramanathan, computational biologist at Argonne National Laboratory, use AI to simulate how the spike protein behaves and gains access to human cells (Peckham, 2021). COVID-19 vaccines are examples of cutting-edge technology. For example, Pfizer and Moderna shots are based on a newer technology that delivers genetic code through molecules known as *messenger RNA* (Zuckerman & Loftus, 2021).

Capturing the First Black Hole Image

The algorithm Katie Bouman started creating as a graduate student at the Massachusetts Institute of Technology (MIT; Shu, 2019) and later as a member of the Event Horizon Telescope team led to the breakthrough first image of the black hole M87 in 2019 (Shu, 2019). The algorithm combines data from eight radio telescopes around the world. Since signals from space reach the telescopes at different rates, mathematical calculations help keep the image accurate (Shu, 2019).

The black hole image helps illustrate the accuracy of Albert Einstein's theory of general relativity, and astronomers and scientists believe the image is one of the most important scientific achievements of the 21st century (Reuell, 2019). This discovery has also ushered in a new era of astronomy. For instance, in 2022, the team captured the first image of Sagittarius A, a supermassive black hole in the center of the Milky Way galaxy, which scientists first suspected existed in the 1960s (O'Callaghan, 2022). Describing integrated STEM, Bouman states, "We're a melting pot of astronomers, physicists, mathematicians and engineers, and that's what it took to achieve something once thought impossible" (Shu, 2019).

Visualizing Cells to Accelerate Drug Discovery

Computational biologist Anne Carpenter started coding out of necessity (Landhuis, 2021). She is senior director of the Imaging Platform at the Broad Institute of MIT and Harvard University, where her team developed CellProfiler, an open-source software for measuring phenotypes (sets of observable traits) from cell images (Landhuis, 2021). Carpenter said during an interview with *Quanta Magazine*, "If you had told college-aged Anne, '22 years from now, you're going to be leading a research group focused on AI,' I would have said you're insane" (Landhuis, 2021).

Scientists characterize stacks of individual cells in microscopy images and attempt to find patterns in the thousands of visualizable cellular properties. They can use these patterns to help identify drugs to fight off viruses in cells. Instead of manually capturing thousands of microscopy images, Carpenter decided to automate the microscope, even though she had no formal training in computer science. This development led her to image analysis and her work to "accelerate biology by working on high-throughput imaging" (Landhuis, 2021).

What You Can Do Now

Real-world application of STEM allows students to see their learning applied in authentic contexts. Therefore, STEM isn't a curriculum and can't be separated from STEM pedagogy (discussed in detail in later chapters). It is difficult for students to become engaged and motivated to learn STEM, or any school subject, if they know nothing about STEM or never see examples of STEM being applied in the real world (Guzdial, 2016). So, what creates the spark of interest, the inspiration, for students as they are initially exposed to STEM? This complicated question doesn't have a succinct answer. However, we teachers can say with some confidence that students are less likely to want to pursue STEM if they don't see examples of people like them succeeding in STEM and if the activities that they are doing in school do not align with the world outside of school (Guzdial, 2016). Consider the following as you determine how to emphasize STEM in your teaching.

Determine Where STEM Fits Into Your Curriculum

STEM can fit into formal (in-school) and informal (after-school, extracurricular) educational environments. If your school day is packed, after-school activities are a great way to get started. Start an after-school robotics club or a computer science club, build small race cars or even rockets with an engineering club, or explore nature with an environmental science club. If you are integrating STEM in formal educational settings, don't feel you must begin by integrating all STEM subjects. For example, engage in a STEM practice, like the engineering design process, or in a STEM subject, like mathematics (National Academy of Engineering & National Research Council, 2014).

Start Students' STEM Learning by Teaching About STEM People and Projects

Teaching students about people like Anne Carpenter (Landhuis, 2021) and Rommie Amaro (Peckham, 2021) shows students the relevance and authenticity of their learning. It doesn't require expertise to share STEM accomplishments. Sharing narratives of STEM pioneers, such as those in table 1.2, can lower the barrier to entry for many teachers who may be apprehensive about teaching STEM. Teaching a narrative is a skill most elementary teachers possess.

TABLE 1.2: Examples of STEM Narratives

Person	Description	STEM Connection
Katie Bouman	Created the algorithm used to capture the first image of a black hole (Shu, 2019)	Mathematics and computer science integrated into the field of astronomy
Rommie Amaro	Created an artificial intelligence algorithm to understand movement of the coronavirus and how it enters human cells (Peckham, 2021)	Mathematics and computer science integrated into the fields of science and biology
Uğur Şahin and Özlem Türeci	Cofounded BioNTech, which developed one of the first COVID-19 vaccines (Zuckerman, 2021)	Every part of STEM, from computer modeling the initial vaccine prototypes to engineering a method to deliver the vaccine all over the world

Provide Students With Examples of Authentic STEM Connections

STEM allows students to see how their learning applies to the real world. Consider the following ways to provide students with examples of authentic STEM connections.

- **Parent discussions (kindergarten–grade 3):** Show students the connections between STEM and the real world by inviting parents into class to discuss their jobs. Parents who are involved in STEM fields can show students that STEM is something they all can do.

- **Current event discussions (grades 4–6):** Include discussions of STEM current events in science and mathematics classes. Magazines like *Scientific American*, *Nature*, and *National Geographic* are excellent sources of material. Also, consider using the science sections of major newspapers, like *The Wall Street Journal* and *The Washington Post*. Here are examples of questions that you can use to begin a discussion.

  ▸ What is the big idea in the article?

  ▸ What makes the article important?

  ▸ Are there words specific to STEM in the article that are new to you?

  ▸ Can you connect something from the article to anything you've experienced?

- **Field trips (all grades):** Field trips to local museums and science centers are a great way to show your students the connections between STEM and the real world. Here are some examples of virtual field trips.

  ▸ Innovation Generation (www.innovation-gen.com) allows students to see how experts in the Stanley Black & Decker Makerspace use STEM-related skills to create technological advancements.

  ▸ Internet of Things (www.learntoconserve.com/internet-of-things) explores STEM careers with technology-focused activities.

  ▸ Access Mars (https://accessmars.withgoogle.com) includes information about NASA's Mars rover mission.

- **Bulletin boards and posters:** In most elementary classrooms, teachers place mathematics on the walls and throughout the room. We can do the same for STEM. For example, hang posters of prominent women in STEM (such as Marie Curie, Juliana Rotich, and Mae C. Jemison). Create a bulletin board to show STEM jobs.

- **Books:** Expand your classroom library with books that highlight STEM pioneers and different STEM careers. Here are a few titles to get you started.

▶ The *Questioneers* series by Andrea Beaty (2007, 2013, 2016), illustrated by David Roberts (including *Iggy Peck, Architect*; *Rosie Revere, Engineer*; and *Ada Twist, Scientist*)

▶ The *Ordinary People Change the World* series by Brad Meltzer (2014, 2018), illustrated by Christopher Eliopoulos (including *I Am Amelia Earhart* and *I Am Neil Armstrong*)

▶ *The Girl With a Mind for Math: The Story of Raye Montague* by Julia Finley Mosca (2020), illustrated by Daniel Rieley

▶ *Counting on Katherine: How Katherine Johnson Saved Apollo 13* by Helaine Becker (2018), illustrated by Dow Phumiruk

▶ *Galaxies, Galaxies!* by Gail Gibbons (2018)

▶ *Human Body!* by DK (2017)

▶ *The Hidden Life of a Toad* by Doug Wechsler (2017)

Visit Other Schools to Observe STEM Instruction

Seeing STEM in action can be a great way to find out how you can begin with STEM. The best way for a first-grade teacher to learn about teaching STEM to students is by visiting other first-grade teachers who are teaching STEM. You can develop relationships with these teachers and begin building your own collaborative community.

Have Spaces Dedicated to Exploring, Tinkering, and Iterating

A learning center is a designated area within a classroom that provides students with activities to practice, enrich, or reteach teaching concepts. The center can be a great opportunity to apply science concepts, mathematics concepts, or both across other STEM domains. Some examples of STEM learning centers include the following.

- **Art center:** Experiment with different colors, textures, and perspectives. Create and engineer stable structures. Create pictures and paintings of various mathematics and science topics.

- **Engineering center:** Explore physical science concepts by creating simple machines, unpowered cars, or both.

- **Gardening center:** Create a learning center outside. Study plants and insects and their different shapes and proportions, engineer different tools, and more.

- **Manipulatives center:** Provide students with building materials. Ask students to design and build structures of their choosing from cardboard, plastic, or paper.

Key Takeaways

Seeing integrated STEM in action is inspiring for teachers and students. The following are some key takeaways from this chapter.

- **STEM is more than an acronym:** It is changing our world for the better. Telling the story of STEM will help inspire and engage students.

- **Teaching STEM is helping students understand their world:** STEM is a mirror to our world. Our students learn more about their world when we teach them STEM.

- **Focus on people in STEM:** Tell their stories. These STEM role models can show students that they, too, can be successful in STEM.

CHAPTER 2

Teaching STEM in Elementary School

Tomorrow's inventors and scientists are today's curious young children—as long as those children are given ample chances to explore and are guided by adults equipped to support them.

—Elisabeth R. McClure and colleagues

When I taught my first STEM lesson to sixth-grade students, I felt apprehensive because I never enjoyed teaching inquiry-based science lessons. However, the lesson's task was simple: code a robot to move in a square. I introduced the commands to make the robot move forward and turn. Now, it was up to the students to use the commands to solve the challenge. Unfortunately, I was not much help. I had the solution code, but teaching is more than providing an answer.

During this STEM lesson, I listened to the students' conversations. They were engaged, whereas previously, some students would not participate. The cool factor of working with a robot seemed to motivate the students. In addition, the assignment's challenge helped because it was difficult but not overwhelming for students.

There was no ambiguity in what they were trying to do: make the robot move in a square. However, the students could not solve the challenge in their first attempt—and they were OK with that. They would troubleshoot, adjust, try again, and repeat that process multiple times. I struggled for years teaching collaborative and iterative problem solving to my students, but here they were learning these skills independently in my first STEM lesson.

For the first time, I saw my students displaying the characteristics of engineers. They tinkered, explored, tried alternative methods, and focused on creating a solution. I had previously seen students do this while they played during recess, but I had struggled with bringing the same level of engagement into my classes. However, as the students tried to get their robot to move in a square outlined on the floor, I saw that engagement firsthand.

This chapter explores becoming a STEM teacher and helping all students become STEM learners. Then, it discusses the interdependency of STEM skills, explains what you can do now, and provides key takeaways.

Becoming a STEM Teacher

Effective STEM teaching can come from any teacher. It doesn't require that you came up in education through STEM disciplines. I lacked enthusiasm for teaching STEM because I never saw myself as good at any of the STEM disciplines. More worrisome, many times I heard my students say similar things: "I love to read, but numbers are not my thing."

My attitude toward teaching STEM had nothing to do with STEM's importance in our society. STEM is critical for preparing students to work in the 21st century, knowledge-based economy and ensuring a nation's ability to be innovative (National Academy of Engineering & National Research Council, 2014). However, STEM is not a subject nor a curriculum (National Science Teaching Association, 2020). It is a way for students to engage in science and engineering practices, collaborate, and understand and explore the relevance of what they are learning. STEM should not take time away from other classes. Instead, it should provide students with the means to see the importance of their learning and have ownership over it (National Science Teaching Association, 2020).

Teaching STEM is not about outputs; it is about the *process* itself, and any teacher can do it. Ironically, being a novice helped me during my first STEM lesson because it allowed me to empathize with my students. Instead of giving the students the answer when they were stuck, I had to reason through the problem with them (because I rarely knew the answer myself).

When I started, I knew nothing about robotics, engineering, or coding. I didn't have a PhD in science or mathematics either, but I had no issues teaching those subjects. My main problem was my mindset, not my lack of training. Becoming a STEM teacher requires acknowledging that your lack of experience in concepts like robotics and coding is not necessarily an impediment. It can actually be a benefit if it creates more learner empathy. Part 3 (page 71) goes into more detail about STEM pedagogy.

Understanding Why All Students Can Become STEM Learners

All our students can become STEM learners and eventually work in a STEM career. This statement is not just rooted in an optimistic belief about student potential; it is rooted in what researchers know about how students learn. My previous attitude toward my mathematics and science abilities is an example of a fixed mindset (Dweck, 2017). All my life, I heard other people refer to themselves as good at either mathematics or reading. I planted my flag in the reading camp. However, research shows that our brains are adaptable (Ericsson & Pool, 2016). For example, we do not have a mathematics brain, nor a reading brain. Instead, our brains can adapt, and we can become better at anything (Ericsson & Pool, 2016).

In their book *Peak: Secrets From the New Science of Expertise*, Anders Ericsson and Robert Pool (2016) provide many examples of the adaptability of our brains. Consider the example of navigating London, which is famously tricky to do and makes the job of the city's taxi drivers difficult. This makes London taxi drivers' memory and navigation skills interesting to psychologists (Ericsson & Pool, 2016). Neuroscientist Eleanor A. Maguire of University College London and her colleague Katherine Woollett followed a group of aspiring taxi drivers for four years to study the growth of their hippocampi. Drivers who became licensed saw significant growth in their hippocampi over the four years of the study (Maguire, Woollett, & Spiers, 2006). Those who did not become licensed drivers, or those involved in the study who had nothing to do with the program to become licensed taxi drivers, saw no change in the size of their hippocampi (Maguire et al., 2006).

Another example from *Peak* involves perfect pitch. People perceive perfect pitch as an innate talent. However, the book shares examples of adults who successfully trained to develop perfect pitch (Ericsson & Pool, 2016).

But what about innate talent? Will some people work less hard than others (or hardly at all) to become proficient at a skill? Ericsson and Pool (2016) examine this question within the context of playing chess. They find no correlation between highly skilled adult chess playing and adult IQs. Higher IQs provide an advantage initially, but that advantage diminishes over time (Ericsson & Pool, 2016).

Peak is full of examples and studies illustrating that anyone can learn anything with proper practice and training (Ericsson & Pool, 2016). Genetics do not necessarily predetermine one's ability or inability to do anything.

The examples and research found in *Peak* stand in contrast to beliefs I had when I taught STEM. Throughout my teaching career, I heard many teachers share the same view as mine: people were naturally better at one subject or another. However, teachers must recognize and understand that all students can be proficient STEM learners, and teachers must also communicate this. Unfortunately, even students as young as two years old can form negative attitudes and opinions about their abilities (Sullivan, 2019).

Many young students form negative stereotypes about their STEM abilities. Researchers point to a phenomenon known as *stereotype threat*, which can, for instance, affect girls who lack confidence about their mathematics abilities, making it difficult to change the underrepresentation of women in STEM fields (Sullivan, 2019). Students may be anxious about a task if they perceive that their performance on the task will be seen through the lens of a negative stereotype (Sullivan, 2019). For example, if boys are always the only ones building with construction blocks and being praised for their creations, it can create a stereotype that boys are the only ones good at building with blocks. This could mean a girl in that classroom feels anxious to play with blocks due to the stereotype. However, research also shows early exposure to STEM can eliminate many negative perceptions (McClure et al., 2017), which is a fundamental reason for starting STEM early.

For early exposure to STEM to be successful, teachers must embrace the concept that all students can be successful STEM learners. As *Peak* illustrates, all students can be great at mathematics, writing, or science (Ericsson & Pool, 2016). As teachers, when we hear our peers say a student has a "mathematics brain" (or doesn't), we need to offer a correction. We also need to challenge such statements from our students. Table 2.1 features growth mindset statements that teachers can say when they hear fixed mindset statements related to STEM.

Exploring the Interdependency of STEM Skills

The foundation for future learning is established in the earliest years of life (Cameron, 2018). For early learners, their learning is an interconnected web. For example, elementary-age students need mature executive-function skills for mathematics and reading proficiency. *Executive function* is composed of three components: (1) inhibitory control, (2) working memory, and (3) cognitive flexibility (Cameron, 2018). Furthermore, executive function does not operate in isolation. Fine and gross

TABLE 2.1: Fixed Mindset Statements Versus Growth Mindset Statements Related to STEM

When you hear this . . .	Say this . . .
"I'm not good at mathematics."	"You may be having a hard time with this specific problem. Don't allow that to make you think poorly about your ability to do mathematics. All of us can be great at mathematics."
"I'm not a tech person."	"All of us can learn how to create things with technology. Anyone can do it—no one is born with a tech gene."
"This is hard."	"This is an opportunity to learn something new."
"My solution isn't correct."	"You get to improve your solution and try again."
"I don't like mathematics and science."	"You haven't been exposed to the parts of mathematics and science that you like yet. I have books I haven't liked, but that doesn't mean I don't enjoy reading. So, let's work together to find something that you enjoy."
"I'm not good at building anything."	"With practice, we can get better at anything. We have the potential to do amazing things. There have been many things that I was not very good at when I first started. With practice, I got better, and so can you."

motor skills and spatial reasoning skills all work together with executive function in young learners (Cameron, 2018).

The collaboration between executive function, motor skills, and spatial reasoning is crucial to understand when considering a skill like mathematics literacy. It is not enough for students to recognize numbers. For example, estimating and reasoning about numbers, verbalizing that information, and recognizing and describing patterns are all part of spatial intelligence (Moss, Bruce, Caswell, Flynn, & Hawes, 2016). In addition, students need opportunities to use their motor skills; research repeatedly shows that students learn first with their eyes, bodies, and hands, which is why manipulatives are prevalent in elementary classrooms (Cameron, 2018). But, again, these skills are interdependent—no single activity or cognitive area is the *most* important. Figure 2.1 shows how these skills work together to form the foundation for learning.

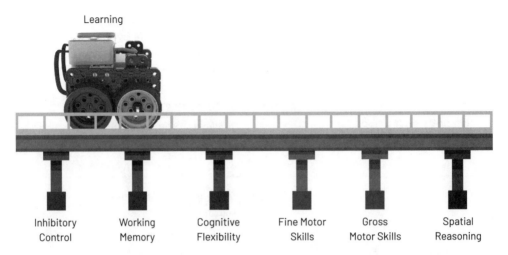

Source: ©2022 VEX Robotics. Used with permission.

FIGURE 2.1: Interconnected skills for building a foundation for future learning.

Consider the earlier example lesson of my students programming a robot to move in a square. For spatial reasoning and motor skills, that construction task was a beautiful activity for mathematics. The process of copying build instructions has enormous benefits for young learners. Researchers identify copying as a visuomotor integration task, meaning students integrate what they see (the build instructions or the finished robot) with what they are doing (building the robot). Visuomotor integration is vital for mathematics and literacy; think of students learning to write their letters (Cameron, 2018).

Throughout the lesson, students discussed how the robot needed to move to complete the test, engaged in peer discussions concerning their progress, and verbalized their thinking. Research tells us that these habits help students with all their cognitive skills (Institute of Medicine & National Research Council, 2015). STEM lessons and pedagogy do not just help students learn STEM; they help students learn *everything*. STEM skills help to create a foundation for all cognitive skills in elementary learners and beyond. Other benefits of starting STEM with elementary students include the following (McClure et al., 2017).

- Early STEM learning leads to better language and literacy outcomes.

- Early STEM learning leads to better listening and reading comprehension.

- Early STEM learning helps students learn how to learn as they age.

As we saw in chapter 1 (page 7), when students learn STEM, they also feel inspired by the world around them. In this sense, STEM learning is a multiplier. The benefits of teaching STEM to young students are abundant and profound.

What You Can Do Now

Don't feel like you need to go all in with STEM immediately. Beginning with a few STEM lessons a month still builds progress. Set goals for emphasizing that all students can learn STEM, incorporating more spatial reasoning into lessons, connecting STEM to your students' world, and beginning a STEM teaching journal.

Find Ways to Incorporate STEM Into Your Elementary Classroom

Find ways to incorporate STEM lessons into your existing science or mathematics classes. Table 2.2 offers a few examples for a first-grade classroom.

TABLE 2.2: Examples of Incorporating STEM Into First-Grade Lessons

Subject	STEM Activity
Science	Investigate stability by having the students create a stable structure using whatever materials you have on hand. For example, choose a classroom character (such as a stuffed animal) and have the students build a chair or a bed for it.
Language Arts	Have students write a story about the character and the structure that they've built.
Mathematics	Have students explore wood pattern blocks or tangrams. Students can expand their spatial reasoning skills by moving and rotating shapes. Ask students to communicate different characteristics of the shapes (their number of sides, their size, similar shapes, and so on).

All these examples can extend beyond first grade. Teachers can have students build stable structures or communicate the characteristics of certain objects across multiple grades. Try incorporating current events that have a STEM theme into your classroom discussions. Also, take advantage of informal educational opportunities. For example, start a STEM club that meets after school. Do a weeklong STEM camp during summer break. Don't try to find the perfect implementation of STEM. Instead, focus on getting started.

Emphasize That All Students Can Learn STEM (or Any Subject)

Provide students with the opportunity to engage in STEM before negative stereotypes take hold. Emphasize that all students can learn anything. Read books and share examples of diversity in STEM fields. Table 2.3 includes a few examples.

TABLE 2.3: Books Highlighting Diversity in STEM Fields

Title	Author	STEM Field
Ada Twist, Scientist (Grades K–2)	Andrea Beaty (2016)	Science
Gary and the Great Inventors: It's Laundry Day! (Grades 3–7)	Akura Marshall (2018)	Engineering
Cece Loves Science (Grades K–3)	Kimberly Derting and Shelli R. Johannes (2020)	Science
The World Is Not a Rectangle: A Portrait of Architect Zaha Hadid (Grades K–5)	Jeanette Winter (2017)	Mathematics
Counting on Katherine: How Katherine Johnson Saved Apollo 13 (Grades K–4)	Helaine Becker (2018)	Mathematics and coding
Zoey and Sassafras: Dragons and Marshmallows (Grades 1–3)	Asia Citro (2017)	Science
Rosie Revere, Engineer (Grades K–2)	Andrea Beaty (2013)	Engineering
Emmy in the Key of Code (Grades 4–6)	Aimee Lucido (2019)	Mathematics and coding

When doing hands-on activities, ensure all students participate equally. Don't shy away from STEM topics. Instead, model your learning and growth for students to show that everyone can learn something new. In addition, you are modeling for students that mistakes and failures are learning opportunities, which can help create a culture of discovery and risk taking. Finally, make sure to correct students (and other teachers) when they say, "I can't learn mathematics," or "I learn mathematics much easier than reading." That thinking can contribute to negative stereotypes.

Incorporate More Spatial Reasoning Into Your Lessons

Since spatial reasoning has a strong correlation with mathematics proficiency, providing students with opportunities to improve their spatial reasoning can pay dividends. A great way to improve spatial reasoning is to have students participate in construction tasks. Examples of construction tasks include the following.

- Coloring pages
- Cutting with scissors
- Building with classroom materials (for example, blocks or magnet tiles)
- Sewing
- Creating with clay or Play-Doh
- Working on puzzles

Each of these activities is applicable to multiple grade levels. Also, prompt students to engage in *spatial talk* throughout the school day. For example, describe the size of objects, compare objects, relate the positions of objects (*above, below, across*), and have students describe their mental representation and manipulation of objects they are using. Researchers have identified several categories of spatial talk (Eason & Levine, 2017).

- Shape terms (examples of which include *circle, triangle, rectangle, cone*, and *pyramid*)
- Dimensional adjectives (examples of which include *big, little, long, short, tall, tiny*, and *huge*)
- Spatial feature terms (examples of which include *curvy, edge, side, line, corner, straight*, and *flat*)
- Positional terms (examples of which include *between, into, forward, over, behind, near*, and *far*)
- Spatial transformations (examples of which include *flip, turn, rotate*, and *slide*)

The following tips and examples help promote strong spatial thinking with elementary students.

- When talking about shapes, go beyond labeling them. Talk about the defining features.

  "How do you know this is a hexagon?"

  "How would you describe this shape if it were cut in half?"

- When participating in spatial activities, use spatial talk.

  When doing a jigsaw puzzle with students, tell them, "I know this puzzle piece is a corner piece because it has two flat (or straight) edges."

- Use spatial talk on the playground.

  When students are on the playground, describe their spatial location: "You went over the bridge, and now you are running under the monkey bars!"

  Hide objects on the playground and challenge students to use navigation strategies and spatial language to find the objects. (You can also do this in the classroom on a rainy day!)

- Use spatial talk during read-alouds by describing the book illustrations.

  "Where is the cat in relation to the ball?"

  "What is at the top of the picture?"

- Use gestures (for example, pointing or tracing objects) to help students understand the meaning of spatial words.

  When you say straight edge, *move your finger along such an edge to show your students what* straight *means.*

  Encourage students to gesture when using spatial words. Ask them, "Can you show me with your hands?"

- Incorporate spatial toys in your classroom.

  Use things like blocks and puzzles, and say things like, "Turn that piece around. Place the red block on top of the green one."

  Use shape sorters and manipulatives, and say things like, "Rotate the two triangles together to make one larger triangle.

Place the objects with more than three sides into this container. Where does the circle go?"

- Ask questions and play games to help students discuss shapes and space.

   Ask students to find specific shapes in the classroom or on the playground. Follow up by asking questions such as, "How do you know that's a square?"

   Tell students that you are thinking of something in the classroom, and have them ask questions to guess what it is. Ask them to use spatial words to figure out the answer (for example, "Is it taller than the desk? Is it behind the library center?").

Describing mental representations and manipulations can help students with their executive-function skills.

Connect STEM to Students' World

Teachers must make connections between STEM subjects explicit to students (National Academy of Engineering & National Research Council, 2014). Create a bulletin board in your classroom of STEM current events. Have students in grades 4–6 provide newspaper clippings of STEM-related articles or pictures. Magazines like *WIRED* and *Scientific American* are excellent sources of information. Discussions about this information can provide students more opportunities to consider diverse role models in STEM and various STEM careers.

You can also provide students with a survey to gauge their thoughts on and interests in STEM and potential STEM careers. Teachers can use the survey in figure 2.2 (page 30) with grades 4–6 students, but they can easily adapt it for younger students.

If students strongly agree that they may choose a career in mathematics or science, you can help them find and explore different careers in those disciplines. This methodology can apply to any of the statements. You can use survey results when pairing students for group work—pair students who show similar interests.

Begin a STEM Teaching Journal

Engineers use their engineering journals daily to track what went well and what didn't. Teachers can also find keeping a journal helpful to record what is going on in their STEM classes. If you are having difficulty thinking of what to write, consider the following questions.

STATEMENTS	STRONGLY DISAGREE				STRONGLY AGREE
	1	2	3	4	5
I like to imagine creating new products.					
I am good at fixing and building things.					
I am curious about how things work.					
I like being creative.					
I might choose a career in science.					
I might choose a career in mathematics.					
I like to help others do their best.					

FIGURE 2.2: Sample student survey.

*Visit **go.SolutionTree.com/instruction** for a free reproducible version of this figure.*

- What was your teaching objective?
- How did class begin?
- How did class end?
- What did you or your students find frustrating during the lesson?
- What went well during the lesson?

Keeping a journal can help you organize your thoughts and reflect on your STEM teaching, which can help you improve your STEM practice as you move forward. It can also serve as a way to collaborate with other STEM teachers.

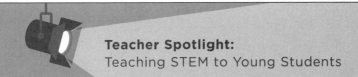

Teacher Spotlight:
Teaching STEM to Young Students

Anna V. Blake teaches STEM across multiple grade levels (K–6) in the Elizabeth Forward School District in Elizabeth, Pennsylvania. In 2021, she received the Most Inspiring Educator award from the Carnegie Science Center in Pittsburgh, Pennsylvania. Blake is coauthor of *Capturing Creativity: 20 Easy Ways to Bring Low-Tech STEAM Into Your Classroom* (Unger & Blake, 2021). The following is an interview with Blake about her experiences teaching STEM (A. Blake, personal communication, December 5, 2021).

Why do you feel it is important to introduce STEM to K–3 students?

STEM started as early as possible allows students to gain agency in their own abilities, especially with hands-on learning. Giving young students agency allows them to understand that they can build and explore using their own abilities such as problem solving, communication, and more in-depth skills like spatial reasoning.

In my experience, I have found that the earlier a child can problem solve, the more confidence a child has in their problem-solving skills later in life. No matter how small the STEM activity, challenge, or lesson, students get the opportunity to solve open-ended problems, which steer away from classic school activities such as using a worksheet or solving a simple addition problem. STEM allows students to solve problems in different ways. I have found that it's fascinating to allow students to share their different solutions to a STEM problem, allowing all students to see how their peers think and problem solve.

How do you deal with students who may have a negative attitude toward STEM (for example, "I'm not a mathematics person")?

I hope to see the negativity toward mathematics, science, and technology dissipate because STEM is viewed as important or taught in early childhood education. A student who is first interacting with STEM at a later age might exhibit frustration. So, I think humor and positivity help in these situations. Although STEM can be the most challenging class in an elementary classroom, it is also the safest place to fail. By showing students that it's OK to fail, I have found that frustration and anger fade into curiosity to solve the problem.

If an elementary school teacher asked how to begin implementing STEM, what advice would you provide?

My advice would be to start small. I love to start the year with a simple STEM challenge like making a paper airplane. This low-entry activity allows me to get to know my students and allows students to feel

continued →

confident and have fun. I want my students to get to know my expectations with a familiar activity.

Describe what you feel are the characteristics of a great STEM lesson.

An excellent STEM lesson must first be fun and then challenging. I find that fun needs to happen first. Students need to engage with something they are interested in or something that is authentic to their own lives. A worksheet gives you everything at once. A STEM lesson adds some mystery, which leads students to want to solve it.

The second part of a great STEM lesson is the challenge. Knowing your students will help you decide how challenging a lesson will be. Ultimately, I like to give my students a challenge that frustrates them and gives each student a sense of accomplishment. The challenge turns a good STEM lesson into a great STEM lesson.

What can you do to encourage students to take risks and view failure as an opportunity to learn more?

I like to cheer on failure and allow students to teach others in the classroom about what didn't turn out well. For example, I had one student working on building a boat. He tested his boat in the water, and it didn't float. He made observations that his boat was leaking. I asked another student to share his observations. Allowing students to share their failures gives students the confidence to try out-of-the-box ideas.

Building this culture of accepting failure in a classroom starts on day one. Allowing students to celebrate successes and failures helps students value trying and challenging themselves. Throughout my teaching career, I have found that students who take risks land on their feet more often than expected. I think gaining that confidence as a child is the best tool to carry on to middle and high school.

What impact has STEM learning had on students in their other classes?

STEM learning has increased my students' confidence in their own abilities. Some students are better at different aspects, such as spatial awareness or problem solving with their hands. Building that confidence increases a student's ability to communicate that skill with others. I have found students who started gaining confidence in their ability in first grade can eventually relay a story about that in fifth grade. Giving students those experiences of accomplishing a difficult challenge is a magical moment.

Why do you love teaching STEM?

STEM allows my students to grow as human beings and gives them confidence in their problem-solving abilities from year to year. By collaborating with middle school and high school teachers, I hear how students come to their classrooms more confident in their abilities to take risks each year.

Key Takeaways

All teachers can teach STEM. The following are some key takeaways from this chapter.

- **STEM starts early:** Young students must be exposed to STEM before they form negative opinions about their STEM abilities.

- **STEM lessons and pedagogy help students learn everything, not just STEM:** STEM skills help create the foundation for all cognitive skills in young learners.

- **All students can be STEM learners:** As teachers, we must remind our students that all of them can become STEM learners.

Part 2

Discover

STEM

Learning
Principles

In addition to being an interdisciplinary approach to learning, STEM is a pedagogy. Part 2 examines learning principles of STEM and provides practical tips, techniques, and procedures that you can begin implementing today. Great teaching transcends a specific domain. The following chapters are applicable not just to STEM lessons but to all teaching.

CHAPTER 3

Focusing on Authentic Engagement, Choice, and Collaboration

To modify motivation, we must change what our students see and what they perceive as normal, acceptable values.

—Doug Lemov

Some of the best advice I ever received as a young teacher was that the best behavior plan is an engaging lesson. As teachers, we strive to engage our students by creating more dynamic (and fun) lessons that lead to higher student learning. Thus, engagement is important—but what is it? How exactly do we define student engagement?

This chapter includes strategies to build motivation, which is a prerequisite for student engagement. It also explains why student choice is essential and how choice boards can help. Then, it discusses how to manage a classroom while maintaining student motivation. Finally, it explores why group work works.

Motivating Students

Student engagement has three dimensions: (1) behavioral, (2) emotional, and (3) cognitive. Table 3.1 (page 38) shows example student actions in each dimension (Nayir, 2017).

TABLE 3.1: Three Dimensions of Student Engagement

Dimension	Student Actions
Behavioral	• Participates in class • Shows effort in class • Is on task • Complies with classroom rules
Emotional	• Has a positive attitude • Is happy • Shows enjoyment when engaging in activities
Cognitive	• Shows resilience and persistence • Shows a willingness to give effort • Is thoughtful

A prerequisite for student engagement is motivation (Nayir, 2017). Unfortunately, motivation is complex and invisible, making it difficult to understand (Mccrea, 2020). Anyone who has spent time in a classroom knows that motivation varies among students. Motivation also isn't fixed. A student may be highly motivated by one lesson but apathetic toward another, which creates a massive challenge for teachers. How do we motivate our students when motivation is hidden and so variable? In *Motivated Teaching: Harnessing the Science of Motivation to Boost Attention and Effort in the Classroom*, learning design expert Peps Mccrea (2020) offers five core drivers of motivation that help teachers understand student motivation.

1. Secure success.
2. Run routines.
3. Nudge norms.
4. Build belonging.
5. Boost buy-in.

Each of these drivers, which I detail in the following sections, can help us think about student motivation and how we can organize and design STEM lessons that foster student engagement.

Secure Success

Solving problems can motivate you; however, working on a problem with the sense that you are failing is not motivating (Willingham, 2021b). Productive struggle that has incremental, even slow, successes can maintain students' motivation.

However, once maintaining momentum seems difficult, or students get confused about how to get started, motivation can wane. STEM lessons with the following characteristics can avoid this sense of failure.

- **Identify and share the lesson's goal or success with the teacher and student:** Sometimes, the teacher and the student can have different interpretations of what success looks like with a lesson. Therefore, if you ask your third-grade students to build a Mars buggy, provide an example of what the buggy could look like, such as figure 3.1.

Source: ©2022 VEX Robotics. Used with permission.

FIGURE 3.1: Example Mars buggy.

- **Ensure that students have the prerequisite skills to successfully complete the activity:** Without the prerequisite skills, students trying to learn and apply a new concept in an open-ended activity may be unsuccessful. The skills must come first. For example, fifth-grade students can combine mathematics and coding to code a robot to move a precise distance. First, they must measure the distance the robot needs to travel. Next, they must determine how many wheel turns to code for the robot to move that distance. They use the two known quantities— (1) distance and (2) wheel circumference—to determine the unknown quantity, which is the number of wheel turns needed. This activity requires the following specific skills.

  ▶ Students must be able to measure.

  ▶ Students need to understand wheel circumference.

  ▶ Students need to be able to multiply and divide whole numbers and decimals.

- **Ensure that the activity is robust:** Students need a clear definition of success, clear instructions, and the necessary skills to complete the lesson. However, the activity needs to allow students to solve problems in different ways. Giving students the opportunity to choose their problem-solving method can create a very motivating sense of ownership (Dueck, 2021). Engineering activities lend themselves well to this principle. Many ways exist to build something (such as a bridge, a stable structure, or the tallest tower) within a wide range of complexities. This variety allows beginning users to succeed immediately, while more experienced users can explore more robust solutions.

Run Routines

Many elementary classrooms have classroom routines. Often, these routines revolve around classroom logistics: exiting the classroom, putting away belongings, doing morning work, and so on. These routines need to extend to STEM activities so that the focus remains on learning. Because STEM activities can sometimes take multiple days, having a clear routine for students to communicate their questions, track their progress daily, make collaborative decisions, and more can help keep the focus on learning and not on procedures. When creating routines, we teachers must keep two things in mind (Mccrea, 2020).

1. What exactly do we want our students to do?
2. What will students need to start and end routines?

When identifying routines for what you want your students to do, look at the list from a student's perspective. Referencing the preceding example of securing success, have you made it clear for students what successfully accomplishing each procedure looks like? For instance, the last activity fifth- or sixth-grade students may do in a robotics class is to write in their engineering notebook. However, only instructing students to log an entry in an engineering notebook isn't clear. Are two sentences an entry? What should the entry capture? When should students begin the engineering notebook entry? To provide better instructions, you could establish a routine like the following.

- When your classroom timer goes off with ten minutes left in class, that is the cue for students to begin writing in their engineering notebook.
- Students write two or three sentences in the engineering notebook that answer these questions.
  - What was one thing your group did well today?
  - What was one thing you changed in the design of the build?

The preceding example also illustrates another important aspect of creating routines—the transition. This example uses a classroom timer, which is a good cue because it is distinct. You could supplement the timer's sound by having the students do something with their hands. For example, everyone might raise their hands when they hear the classroom timer. This action makes the auditory cue easier for all students to recognize.

Nudge Norms

I've been in many parent-teacher conferences where parents were amazed at how polite, hardworking, and diligent their children were in my classroom. They would tell me how much they struggled to get their children to do simple chores at home, but I reported that the students were always on task in my classroom. As much as I would love to attribute the students' behavior to some amazing trick or technique, often the cause was my having norms. The students perceived school as a place to learn and do certain tasks. The students did not feel the same about home, which could be attributed to any number of reasons, none of which speak poorly of anyone's parenting.

As you'll learn more about in chapter 4 (page 55), a classroom culture needs to reward failure and use norms to guide behavior. Norms in classrooms can work with learning goals or against them. Keep in mind that students are motivated toward actions that appear highly valued by the teacher and easy to accomplish in the classroom (Mccrea, 2020).

Therefore, if we want students to participate, explore multiple ways to solve problems, and act thoughtfully, we need to elevate the visibility of the norms that guide the behavior. For example, build routines in your classroom to recognize students who have exhibited positive behaviors that are within classroom norms—or even better, have the students recognize one another during classroom discussions or perform actions of recognition (for example, tap their desk or snap their fingers). Some routines to nudge norms are shown in table 3.2 (page 42).

Build Belonging

Students are motivated to be part of a group because they want to belong. In *The Tactical Teacher: Proven Strategies to Positively Influence Student Learning and Classroom Behavior*, Dale Ripley (2022) says:

> Students have a strong need to belong to various peer groups and know where they fit within these groups. Teachers can use this desire to belong both to motivate students and to set appropriate boundaries for their students' in-school behaviors. (p. 15)

TABLE 3.2: Example Routines to Nudge Norms

Routine	Explanation	Grade Levels
No Opt Out	Remind students that they shouldn't answer, "I don't know." No opt out is a positive way to remind students to always try to provide an answer.	All grade levels
Cold Call	Cold call is a technique for a teacher to call on students randomly. It is a great way to ensure all students understand a lesson. Frame cold call in a positive, not punitive, way.	All grade levels
Post It	Post the clear criteria for success as a constant reference and reminder.	All grade levels
Tight Transitions	Tight transitions decrease the time used to transition from one activity to the next and increase the teaching time available. This routine also leads to less frustration for students. Create a tight transition by using a song (such as a memorable cleanup song), using a rhyme, or asking students to make a physical gesture. A teacher can combine these methods (for example, when students hear a song, they raise both hands).	Grades K–2
SLANT	*SLANT* stands for *sit up, lean forward, ask questions, nod your head,* and *track the speaker*. This routine is a great way to remind students of what engagement looks like in a classroom. Use the SLANT acronym as a quick reminder when students aren't sitting up, tracking a speaker, and so on.	Grades 4–6

Source: Adapted from Lemov, 2021.

When I coached high school football, I used the desire to belong to motivate students. It seemed to me that students would do anything for a T-shirt, so I created T-shirts for reaching different milestones. If students came to a certain number of consecutive workouts or reached a specific goal, they got a T-shirt. Unfortunately, it was always difficult to order the right number of shirts in the correct sizes. Inevitably, one student would end up with a shirt two or three sizes too big. It didn't matter.

They wore the shirt with pride, which left a lasting impact on me. The T-shirts represented belonging.

Since building a sense of belonging fosters student motivation, teachers should strive to build belonging in their classrooms. The more that students identify with one another, the more that they will feel confident in your classroom's generation of desired opportunities and outcomes (Mccrea, 2020).

You can easily build a sense of belonging if your classroom has an identity. For example, the T-shirts constantly communicated an aspect of the football team's identity. The back of each T-shirt had the following text.

TEAM
Me

Big *team*, little *me*. The team's identity was all about unselfishness and teamwork. For K–3 classrooms, the identity could be that all students can succeed at STEM. You can enhance this identity by hanging signs all over the classroom that say:

WELCOME TO MR. McKENNA'S ROOM
Where *all* students succeed in STEM

In grades 4–6, you can emphasize traits like perseverance. For example, make *can't* a banned word in your classroom, and have students replace it with *not yet able to*.

Other tips for building a classroom identity include the following.

- **Find commonalities among the students:** Emphasize that students all share some common likes, interests, hobbies, and so on.

- **Establish a unifying purpose (Mccrea, 2020):** Allow students to rally around a classroom challenge or activity. When talking with students, use words like *we* and *us*. Take the time to recognize all students for something, which will help everyone feel like they are part of the collective classroom identity.

- **Create a classroom charter:** With your students, create a list of values that your class will attempt to personify. For example, one of the values might be empathy. When students show empathy toward one another, you can highlight your classroom charter. Having the classroom charter can help build the classroom identity.

- **Create a bulletin board of your students:** Make a bulletin board featuring pictures of your students and information about them. Include information about what they enjoy most about your classroom. This is another great way to build commonality among your students.

Boost Buy-In

Providing students with choices can be highly motivating for them (Merrill & Gonser, 2021). One of the most rewarding aspects of my job is interacting with students during VEX Robotics competitions. As I discussed in the introduction (page 1), these competitions are full of highly engaged and motivated students, so there is a lot of buy-in. At first glance, you might think the desire to win motivates these students. That may be true to a certain extent, but their buy-in goes deeper.

At the competitions, I hear students discuss the design of their robots, and I watch as they explain their code. I listen as they discuss their strategies to try to get as many points as possible. They are describing their choices.

Providing students with choices can be highly motivating for them (Merrill & Gonser, 2021). Student choice does not entail a pure democracy where students vote on everything that happens in a classroom. Instead, *student choice* means providing students with some autonomy when they are completing an open-ended challenge. Differentiated instruction expert Jane A. G. Kise (2021) says, "Remember that students learn to make good decisions only through the experience of making decisions. They can't mature without some autonomy" (p. 59). Therefore, choice fits terrifically with STEM when you make the success criteria clear to the students and allow them to iterate their way to a solution.

EXAMPLES OF STUDENT CHOICE IN GRADES K–3

Having a large number of simple, student-facing STEM activities in a classroom STEM learning center allows you to offer time for students to choose an activity. Therefore, this strategy requires making time for the learning center. Provide STEM activities that are robust enough to have multiple solutions. Anything from coding a robot to move in a square to building a tower with toothpicks or plastic construction pieces can help the students iterate their way to solutions.

You can conduct classroom competitions that foster student choice and emphasize cooperation and collaboration instead of competitiveness. In addition, you can ask students to choose STEM role models to study.

EXAMPLES OF STUDENT CHOICE IN GRADES 4–6

Give students a say when creating classroom norms (Merrill & Gonser, 2021). These norms can be part of building the classroom identity. Also, provide students with a choice in assessment and with opportunities to choose whom to work with and where to sit within the classroom. Chapter 6 (page 91) provides more details on why cocreating learning targets with students is a powerful example of student choice (Dueck, 2021).

Another idea for boosting buy-in is to use choice boards, which are bulletin boards, either physical or virtual, that allow students to learn in different ways about a particular topic. You can use choice boards in all grades in multiple ways, such as the following.

- Engage students who finish early.

- Assess what students have learned at different points throughout the unit.

- Extend the unit or lesson.

- Allow students to display and share their thinking and learning.

The STEM choice board provides content that you can add to the classroom's existing choice board or to any classroom's bulletin board.

EXAMPLE OF A GRADES K-3 CHOICE BOARD

You could use the choice board in figure 3.2 in a K–3 classroom that is getting started with robotics and coding.

Story in Pictures	**Human Code**	**Find the Bug**
Create picture cards to represent a daily activity or routine, like brushing your teeth. Then, place the cards on the floor and make your robot move to each step in order.	With a partner, decide who will be the coder and who will be the robot. Using classroom materials, create a short maze for the robot to navigate. The coder will then tell their partner how to move to escape the maze.	List the commands to make the robot move forward five spaces, turn left, and move three spaces in an incorrect order. Ask a friend to find the bug and fix it by putting the commands in the correct order.
Invent a Programming Language	**Behavior Bingo**	**Make a Sequence Puzzle**
Imagine you are the robot. What command would make you move forward one step, turn left, turn right, or make a sound? Write or draw the commands for those four actions, and give them to a friend to see if they can code you.	Make a bingo card with different behaviors you do at home or school. Then, at the end of the day, play behavior bingo and check off how many of those behaviors you did during the day. Did you get five in a row?	Draw or write four or five steps you take to do a task in your classroom, like sharpen a pencil. Then cut them out. Mix them up and give them to your partner to put in the correct order.

FIGURE 3.2: Example grades K-3 choice board.

EXAMPLE OF A GRADES 4-6 CHOICE BOARD

You could use the choice board in figure 3.3 in a grades 4–6 classroom embarking on an engineering unit on simple machines.

Measuring With Pieces	**Matching Game**	**Draw It**
How many construction pieces does it take to go across one sheet of paper? First guess, then test.	Can you match two builds together that use the same pieces but in different patterns?	Can you find any shapes in the room that match the shapes of your construction pieces? How do you know they are the same shape? Use spatial talk.
Gears	**Photographer**	**Simple Machine Scavenger Hunt**
How many gears can you mesh together? Use gears and axles to build a contraption.	Take pictures of real-life simple machines from your house, your neighborhood, or both. Label what type of simple machine each is, and identify what it does.	How many of these simple machines can students find in the room, in the school, and at home: inclined plane, lever, wheel and axle, and gear?

FIGURE 3.3: Example grades 4-6 choice board.

No matter the grade level, you can also cocreate choice boards with students, thus providing more opportunities for students to share what they have learned in different ways. Choice boards can start with two or three choices and add more as students provide input on how they can share their learning. More information on making assessment more student centered is found in chapter 6 (page 91). Choice boards can take the place of other forms of summative assessment.

Understanding How Classroom Management Affects Student Motivation

Teachers' opinions vary on the look of a well-managed classroom. Some teachers have classrooms where they do most of the talking and students sit quietly in rows. Other teachers do little talking, and their classrooms buzz with students moving, talking, and sharing. In many STEM classrooms, students move freely throughout the room, talking and making messes—all with the approval of their teacher. Some of these teachers employ flexible seating, which makes their classroom look more like a Starbucks than a traditional classroom.

Which is the best managed classroom? Based on outward appearances, it is difficult to say. Moreover, what does *managed* even mean? Projects and resources are managed, but are classrooms? Are students? When we say *classroom management*, what are we trying to communicate?

A classroom full of students who are off task and disruptive is daunting for any teacher. Creating a highly engaged classroom is the best way to avoid that situation. Consider also that a classroom full of students sitting passively at their desks for hours of direct teacher instruction is not the same as a classroom full of students engaging with their learning. The goal is *learning*. Therefore, instead of discussing classroom management, it is better to discuss motivating students and fostering engagement. This gets to the core message of the quote from educator Doug Lemov (2021) that started this chapter: "To modify motivation, we must change what our students see and what they perceive as normal, acceptable values" (p. 25).

Many middle and high school students view apathy as the default mode for school, while most kindergarten and first-grade classrooms are full of energy and enthusiasm. Unfortunately, energy and enthusiasm wane as students get older (Calderon & Yu, 2017). Soon disengagement and apathy become the norm. Nothing is sadder than a student afraid to show interest in a subject for fear of failure or mockery by their peers.

Therefore, teachers want to create a classroom environment where students are enthusiastic about their learning, find their learning interesting and important, and feel they can do the learning activities. Moreover, teachers want students to feel empowered and show their enthusiasm and interest because that is what is valued and expected in their classroom. Chapter 4 (page 55) is devoted to discussing effective classroom culture.

Collaborating to Enhance Learning

Teachers often ask students to solve problems, tasks, and challenges in groups. This type of learning mirrors how learning often occurs for many adults. For example, in the workplace, adults learn through highly contextualized experiences such as working in groups. Therefore, employing group work and engaging students in authentic tasks prepare them for the workplace.

Learning incidentally or effortlessly is a goal in our classrooms. Incidental learning happens when learning is situated as part of the activity, context, and culture where the learning is developed and used; this process is called *situated learning* (Kirschner & Hendrick, 2020). Situated learning can seem complex, but it is a simple concept that most people have seen or experienced. For example, think of a child engrossed in a game. The child is learning, and that learning is situated. Also, the learning occurs incidentally and within an appropriate context (playing the game).

Situated learning depends on culture (chapter 4, page 55) and collaboration (Kirschner & Hendrick, 2020). While working in a group, students discuss their thinking, so their sense making becomes social. When embedded into an authentic context (like a real-world STEM challenge), this collaboration can be natural, and the learning is incidental. Again, this is how learning often happens in every-day situations.

With situated learning, be mindful to ensure that students' activities are embedded within an authentic context. You can create a classroom expectation that everyone needs to participate in group work. However, is this effective without also model-ing effective group collaboration? Also, if students collaborate only to comply, is that effective?

The first goal of situated learning is to engage students in authentic tasks where collaboration occurs as a direct result of the tasks. The task design, as detailed in Motivating Students (page 37), is essential to effective student collaboration. In robotics competitions, students are prompted to participate, stay on task, or share tasks equally. These competitions are great examples of students collaborating and learning incidentally within the context of how that learning is used. The critical consideration is the robustness of the activity, which you can analyze by asking your-self questions like the following.

- Will students view the activity as engaging and fun?

- Is the activity robust enough that all students will have an active role?

- Does the activity have clear directions and outcomes?

- Does the activity allow for multiple solutions?

- Does the activity account for different student interests?

Not all activities can reach each of these goals, but the more robustness that activi-ties incorporate, and the more of these engagement boxes you can check, the better. Therefore, the design of an activity that involves group work is important. Here are some other ideas for getting the most out of group work.

- **Teach collaborative problem solving:** Communication needs to be taught and reinforced for students to do it well. Teach your students the following skills.

> ▶ *Listen actively*—Don't interrupt when someone is talking. Instead, give your full attention by sitting up, leaning forward, and nodding to acknowledge the speaker.

> ▶ *Ask questions*—If you're unsure of an idea from a classmate, repeat what you think they meant or are suggesting. Don't just say, "I'm not sure what you mean."

> ▶ *Disagree productively*—Eventually, the group may need to come to a compromise or vote on a strategy. That's OK because productively disagreeing can lead to wonderful ideas. This kind of disagreement often happens in the workplace. Use a calm voice when trying to decide whose idea to utilize.

Spend a few minutes at the end of each class recognizing examples of active listening, questioning, and productive disagreement.

- **Teach persistence:** Persistence is a valuable skill for school and life. Documenting persistence is an essential way to reinforce the practice of persistence with your students while emphasizing it as a shared value in your classroom and school. For students in grades K–3, create a *looks like, feels like, sounds like* display on the idea of persisting. Have students contribute to each section; they can add specific examples from their own learning for several weeks. Then, take time to discuss the examples with students. Figure 3.4 shows an example bulletin board for K–3 students with sample student text.

PERSISTENCE		
Looks Like	Feels Like	Sounds Like
I was able to stay on task for the entire class period.	Wow! Our code made the robot finally get through the entire maze!	I talked with Lisa about the best way to change our design after the first attempt didn't go as we planned.

FIGURE 3.4: Example of a persistence bulletin board.

For older students, create a persistence concept map, such as figure 3.5 (page 50). You can add to the concept map throughout the group activity.

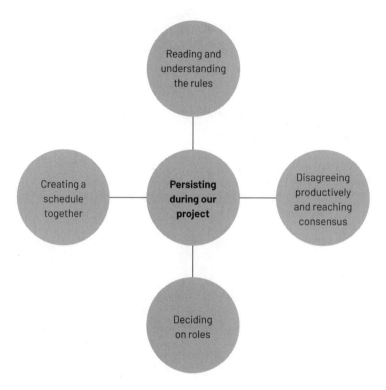

FIGURE 3.5: Example of a persistence concept map.

- **Provide structure:** Make sure students understand what success means for the activity and the rules they need to follow to achieve that success. Don't assume that students will understand. Model effective group communication and procedures; use a formative assessment, such as an exit ticket, to make sure students understand the rules. And have the students explain to you what success for the project means. Remind them throughout the activity.

What You Can Do Now

Motivation is a prerequisite for student engagement. By understanding and using the five drivers of motivation, teachers can improve student engagement in their classrooms. In addition, teachers can provide authentic connections, use random rewards, and spread classroom values to build engagement.

Use the Five Drivers of Student Motivation

Using the five drivers of student motivation (secure success, run routines, nudge norms, build belonging, and boost buy-in) does more for classroom management than anything else. Student motivation leads to student engagement, which leads to excellent behavior from students.

Provide Students With Authentic Connections

A mistake when teaching STEM is emphasizing the need to fill future STEM jobs. Future jobs are not authentic connections for students. Students aren't interested in learning things that don't have real-world applications today. They want experiences that are authentic in practice, and they want some ownership and choice in their learning (Dueck, 2021). Here are examples of STEM activities that connect to the real world.

- **Mars rover-surface operations (VEX GO Labs, n.d.b):** This activity is modeled after NASA's Mars 2020 mission. Teachers ask students to build and code a robot that mimics the mission of the Mars rover. This activity works well in grades 4–6.

- **Sailing adventure:** This activity is great for K–3 students; teachers can use it with a story from a language arts lesson. Students build a sail and code their robot to move with the sail to get to buried treasure.

Use Random Rewards

Making rewards random and intermittent for your students helps keep them engaged during lessons and activities. Some ideas for random rewards include the following.

GRADES K–3

- Surprise the class with an ice cream party. Do this after all the students have completed a few challenges.

- Randomly give students stickers for exemplary work.

- Print certificates for certain achievements and randomly give them to students.

GRADES 4–6

- Randomly provide tickets for good behavior. When students collect a certain number of tickets, allow them to get a prize from the class store.

- Randomly throughout the year, call home to share a great thing a student did in the classroom with the student's parents. This practice also helps you form strong bonds with parents.

- Give notes with encouraging messages. Messages can be simple, such as, "You did a great job listening to your group today." You can put these on sticky notes or email the messages to students.

Spread Classroom Values

The more your classroom values are adopted schoolwide and communicated to the school community, the better. Spreading classroom values reinforces to students that engagement is the norm, not the exception. You can spread classroom values by sending your students' guardians a detailed, content-specific letter about what the students are learning and creating when doing STEM in the classroom. You can also send this letter home to principals and other administrators. The following citations lead to some examples of letters that you can use for inspiration. Each is a Google document that allows for easy editing.

- Grades 1–3 robotics (VEX GO Labs, n.d.a)
- Grades 4–6 robotics (VEX IQ, n.d.)

Teacher Spotlight:
Motivating Students in a STEM Classroom

Colleen Hinrichsen teaches science, technology, engineering, the arts, and mathematics (STEAM) to about 850 second to fourth graders at Mars Area Elementary School in Mars, Pennsylvania. Before teaching STEAM, she frequently and effectively used choice boards with her students as a means for differentiation and engagement. In the following interview, Hinrichsen shares her ideas for motivating students (C. Hinrichsen, personal communication, December 15, 2021).

How did you initially get students excited about a STEM lesson?

Getting students excited about STEM lessons depends on the topic. For computer science topics, I have found that students like to see example projects I have made (or my students have made). I try to choose projects that appeal to different student interests or passions. For robotics lessons, I find videos of robots that are meaningful to students now (like a robot waiter in China). Students find inspiration in watching an amazing video, then breaking down what they saw in STEAM class. They realize that I am teaching them that they can create anything.

Sometimes students like a good challenge or competition, so they are motivated from the start. However, I have found that having two of any challenge is essential. The first challenge allows for learning and experimenting. The second challenge later in the year allows students to learn from their experiences. I often have class-against-class (cumulative-score) competitions rather than individual-versus-individual competitions to keep students from being as competitive with each other.

Do you have any routines in your classroom that help keep students engaged and motivated?

Students are rarely off task in my room. I display something on the big screen to make them curious when they walk in. Also, I try to deliver my lessons so that the students feel like everything is the most important lesson they will learn. I vary maker-style projects with digital projects, so they never get bored. In addition, I tell them they will earn a choice day if they try all the activities in the given weeks. For the most part, my students' own creations (or their classmates') motivate them enough. If they veer from my original plan, they know that is OK. They are always thinking from the start.

When teaching, what do you do to make sure that students stay engaged during the lesson?

I ask students about what they are doing. Most of the time in my class, when students are off task, it is because they are confused and fool around instead of asking for help. When I check in with those students from the start, those behaviors rarely occur. I can get the students back on track or discuss ways to modify a project to make it appealing. They appreciate making projects individualized when possible. The primary way I keep students engaged is to show them that I care about them, I am proud of them, and I am excited to see what they make. If I struggle to keep up with "look at this" moments, I know it is a good day.

Why do you like using choice boards?

Students get some control, and I can see the activities students enjoy, or I can see areas that need a different approach because they are less chosen. Choice boards also allow students to feel ownership of their learning. For example, when I taught third-grade events in coding, I allowed students to choose one track out of three options instead of forcing them to do all three.

How do you use choice boards?

Sometimes, I use them as a reward. Sometimes, I use the boards like bingo—finishing a choice in each category will unlock something else. A favorite is a freestyle maker project (either hands-on or within *Minecraft: Education Edition*).

What tips and strategies would you share with a new teacher trying to create choice boards?

I recommend starting with only a couple of choices. Those choices should be introduced and practiced before students are 100 percent independent. These choices could be brief to get the routine down. Then, each week, add another choice. I also recommend having exemplars or directions already created—even making a little video for

continued →

reference at each choice is a great idea. Some classes need more, so having something to reference (print or video) is key. Finally, it is also fun to gamify choice boards.

Key Takeaways

Engaged students participate and stay on task. The following are some key takeaways from this chapter.

- **Define what success looks like:** Overcommunicate it to your students by providing plenty of examples. Also, ensure students have the skills needed to complete an activity.

- **Use routines:** Routines will help ensure the activity of learning has the right amount of challenge but the process of learning is easy for students.

- **Encourage positive norms:** Find ways to easily and consistently draw attention to positive norms in your classroom.

- **Create a sense of belonging:** Foster a classroom identity that breeds common ground and a sense of belonging for your students.

- **Provide opportunities for student choice:** Create and implement tasks that allow students multiple methods to solve problems.

- **Create a highly engaged classroom:** A highly engaged classroom with motivated students leads to better learning outcomes and productive teachers and students.

CHAPTER 4

Creating Risk Takers

In science, there is no such thing as failure.

—Gregory Zuckerman

The Entertainment Technology Center (ETC) of Carnegie Mellon University is an interdisciplinary research center with a mission to combine art and technology at the core of an applied-research, inquiry-focused education. ETC originally had two codirectors: (1) Randy Pausch (2008), a computer science professor (who later wrote the inspirational book *The Last Lecture*), and (2) Don Marinelli, a drama professor. Embedded in ETC's philosophy is the development of a culture where students feel empowered to take risks.

Raj Balasubramanian attended ETC from 2011 to 2013 to obtain a master's degree in entertainment technology. He is now a senior software engineer at VEX Robotics. He says the following about how ETC empowers students to take risks:

> Every project we worked on at ETC was done with seemingly impossible deadlines—sometimes a week, sometimes two days! It felt like we were constantly playing catch-up with what we originally envisioned. . . . But no one at ETC shoots down an idea, however outrageous it may seem. We were encouraged to see our ideas through, to put in the work necessary. (R. Balasubramanian, personal communication, December 15, 2021)

I once took a group of third- to seventh-grade students for a tour of ETC. There, I saw that every plaque on the wall included a picture of a penguin. These were the First Penguin Awards. Pausch (2008) explains the First Penguin Award in his book *The Last Lecture*:

> When I taught the "Building Virtual Worlds" course, I encouraged students to attempt hard things and to not worry about failing. I wanted to reward that way of thinking. So at the end of each semester, I'd present one team of students with a stuffed animal—a penguin. It was called "The First Penguin Award" and went to the team that took the biggest gamble in trying new ideas or new technology, while failing to achieve their stated goals. In essence, it was an award for "glorious failure," and it celebrated out-of-the-box thinking and using imagination in a daring way. (p. 10)

At that point, I was a veteran teacher of eighteen years. I had been to countless professional learning sessions and visited dozens of other teachers' classrooms. I subscribed to educational journals and newsletters. Yet, never had I seen something as simple yet powerful as the First Penguin Award. I also had never seen "glorious failure" emphasized like this. Rewarding failure—what an incredible but also foreign concept, one I would take back to my classroom. This chapter explores why celebrating failure is critical to creating risk takers. It discusses how failure is integral to the engineering design process, which we teachers can use with students as young as kindergartners.

Viewing Failure as a Goal

If we want students to be iterative and persistent in a STEM lesson, we must cultivate a culture where failure is a goal. It is not enough for us to accept failure as OK.

In *The Innovator's Dilemma: When New Technologies Cause Great Firms to Fail*, Clayton M. Christensen (2016) discusses the importance of failure as it relates to innovation. Christensen says companies that succeed by introducing disruptive technologies to the marketplace can fail because of the same behaviors that made them successful in the first place. Christensen (2016) lists these behaviors.

- Listening to their customers
- Investing aggressively in technology that their customers want
- Seeking higher profits
- Targeting larger markets rather than smaller ones

How can listening to customers lead to failure? As Christensen (2016) explains, what makes new technologies disruptive is that they change the value proposition in a market. As a result, when a disruptive technology is first released, it doesn't have a market. Markets that don't exist can't be analyzed. For example, as children, we were told never to get into a car with strangers. However, that is the entire business model of Uber.

What does this have to do with failure, education, and STEM? Christensen (2016) explains:

> Not only are the market applications for disruptive technologies unknown at the time of their development, they are unknowable. The strategies and plans that managers formulate for confronting disruptive technological change, therefore, should be *plans for learning and discovery rather than plans for execution* [emphasis added]. (p. 143)

The takeaway? Fail fast. Learn fast. Apply new learning. Try again. That's what successful start-ups do to innovate and create disruptive technology. An important aspect of failing fast is not becoming too attached to a particular idea for too long. Balasubramanian notes:

> Most of us tend to get married to the path we are on, the one we have spent hours and days on, the one we are determined to fix, even when a new path might be what we need most. We don't want to give up on what we nurtured, and in doing so, we forget that our goal is to get the most value out of our time. To do this, we must be willing to let go of baggage that doesn't serve us while carrying with us the lessons our attempts taught us. (R. Balasubramanian, personal communication, December 15, 2021)

On the World Economic Forum's list of the top ten job skills (as cited in Whiting, 2020), analytical thinking and innovation come first (see chapter 5, page 75, for the full list). But what does *innovation* mean? How does one innovate? As Christensen (2016) explains, one innovates by emphasizing failure and learning, not executing a process of incremental improvement.

As teachers, how often do we create projects that allow students to fail, learn from that failure, and apply that learning in a subsequent attempt? Probably not often enough. Why is that? Much like in business, where the goal is an incremental increase of profits in established markets, the goal in education is often incremental improvement as reflected by proficiency gains with learning standards. Managers in a company are motivated to improve profits incrementally, and students and teachers are motivated to improve skills incrementally.

Often, the classroom entirely focuses on getting a good grade, not failing fast, learning, and applying new learning. Learning stops when the focus becomes the grade (Wiliam, 2018b). Therefore, we should define the goal as failure, not a grade.

Understanding Failure and the Engineering Design Process

Unlike students, engineers are often encouraged to create open-ended designs to solve problems through continuous improvement and testing. The engineering design process (EDP) removes the stigma from failure because failure is an integral part of problem solving, it leads to critical thinking, and it is a positive way to learn. The EDP consists of three steps.

1. Define the problem.
2. Develop solutions.
3. Optimize.

A Framework for K–12 Science Education (National Research Council, 2012) defines *engineering* as "any engagement in a systematic practice of design to achieve solutions to particular human problems" (p. 437). Let's unpack that definition.

- *Any engagement in a systematic practice of design* is the EDP.
- *Achieve solutions to particular human problems* is what engineers do. It explains the difference between engineers and scientists: engineers create and scientists investigate.

Therefore, engineers use the EDP to create solutions to human problems. The problems are complex, and usually, many solutions exist. However, there is never a perfect solution. Also, the first attempt at a solution is almost always wrong.

Engineers call repeated failure *iteration* partly because it doesn't have the same negative connotation as *failure*. Because we must explicitly make failure a goal in our classrooms, it's vital that we eliminate the negative connotation of failure.

Let's take a closer look at the EDP in different grade bands, starting with grades K–2 in figure 4.1.

Figure 4.1 breaks down the EDP for K–2 students. The *define* step introduces students to problems as situations that people want to change through engineering. Next, students are encouraged to create and share a solution in the *develop solutions* step. In the *optimize* step, students receive feedback on their solution and attempt to improve it. Using terms like *optimize* and *iterate* helps avoid using the term *fail*. In addition, emphasize from the beginning that students' first attempt at a solution will not be their only attempt. Let's look at a project using the EDP in a K–2 classroom.

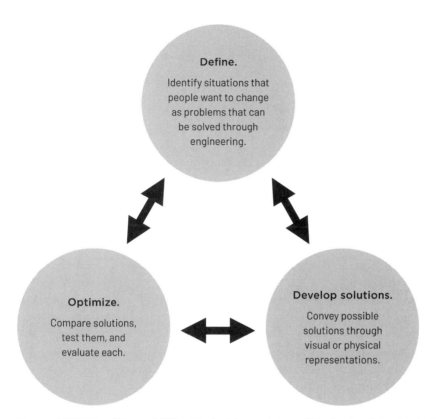

Source: NGSS Lead States, 2013a. Used with permission of The National Academies Press, from Next Generation Science Standards: for States, by States permission conveyed through Copyright Clearance Center, Inc.

FIGURE 4.1: Engineering design process for grades K–2 students.

Grades K–2 Project: Design and Create a Chair or Bed for Your Favorite Stuffed Animal

Bring in a few stuffed animals and tell students that the stuffed animals are exhausted from their journey to school today and want to relax in either a chair or a bed. The students' challenge is to make a chair or bed from classroom supplies (cardboard, tape, wooden craft sticks, construction paper, and so on).

Organize the students into groups of two, (1) a builder and (2) a recorder. Assign the following responsibilities to the group members.

- Builder:
  - ▸ Gathers materials
  - ▸ Builds the first version
  - ▸ Tests and records results on an EDP poster

- Recorder:
  - ▸ Draws an initial design on the EDP poster
  - ▸ Takes apart the first version
  - ▸ Begins building the second version

- Both:
  - ▸ Document the define step in the EDP
  - ▸ Test the design
  - ▸ Follow directions and work together

The roles are balanced so students do not feel that one role is less fair or important than the other. For example, the recorder doesn't only write, and the builder doesn't only build; they take turns.

Before students begin, give them an EDP poster. Here, they can fill out each part of the EDP.

- **Define:** The students write and share what they are trying to do. Many students will immediately try to begin building. This step lets the teacher see that everyone understands the activity's goal before building begins.

  Example—Create a bed for Ducky.

- **Develop solutions:** The recorder draws the initial idea.

- **Optimize:** The builder records the results of the first test and subsequent tests.

  Example—The first bed fell apart. We need to use more glue. The second bed was too sticky with glue.

Notice on the EDP image (figure 4.1, page 59) that students aren't supposed to follow the steps in a prescribed sequence. Instead, students can tweak their first design (develop another solution) and test (optimize) again.

Many students think their first solution is the best one (National Research Council, 2012). Therefore, rewarding the most spectacular attempt (iteration) can help change that habit. The classroom culture needs to reward multiple failures.

Chapter 7 (page 117) discusses STEM and creativity. One aspect discussed is not letting students rush through the design step of the EDP. Students who spend more time on design will be less inclined to fixate on their first solution. You can help students by prompting them with questions like the following.

- What size should the bed or chair be?

- What makes a comfortable bed or chair?

- What is on a bed or chair?

- What style is the bed or chair?

Maybe a group of students will try to make an adjustable bed or bunk bed. Maybe it will fail spectacularly—and that would be great! Would it be better if every group made a basic chair or bed frame? The goal of the activity is not to make a chair or bed. The goal of the activity is to engage with the EDP, which requires multiple attempts. In other words, the goal is failure.

Let's look at the EDP for grades 3–6 (see figure 4.2).

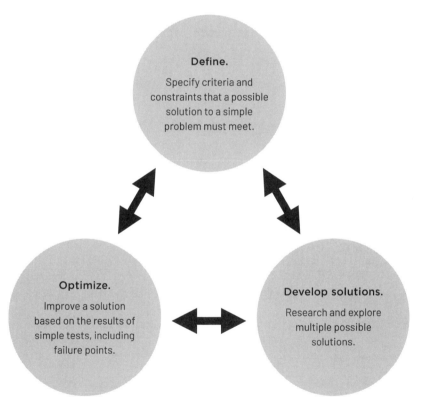

Source: NGSS Lead States, 2013a. Used with permission of The National Academies Press, from Next Generation Science Standards: for States, by States permission conveyed through Copyright Clearance Center, Inc.

FIGURE 4.2: Engineering design process for grades 3–6 students.

You can see that the steps in the EDP are the same as in grades K–2 (see figure 4.1, page 59). The following are the differences for the next level of the EDP.

- Students are expected to identify criteria and constraints.

- Students are expected to identify multiple solutions from the beginning.

- Students then use data from those multiple solutions.

These differences in the EDP introduce to students a key concept that hardware and software engineers deal with all the time: trade-offs. For example, suppose that software engineers develop a video game with amazing graphics. But what if only high-end devices can run the game? The engineers have disqualified most of the game's market. In other words, there is a trade-off between graphics and compatibility. This example illustrates why failing fast is essential. How do the engineers know where to strike that trade-off? The answer is they don't. Instead, they want to deliver a game as fast as possible to the market, collect feedback, and adjust as quickly as possible.

In mechanical engineering, trade-offs often involve cost and time. For example, suppose you were building your house and wanted multiple bedrooms, a guest room, a three-stall garage, and so on. How long would that take to build? How much would it cost? Engineers make these trade-offs every day. Therefore, it is helpful for students to experience working with trade-offs early. Let's look at a project using the EDP in grades 3–6 classrooms.

Grades 3–6 Project: Design and Create a Container for the Egg Drop Challenge

The premise of the egg drop challenge is simple: create a container that keeps a raw chicken egg from cracking when dropped from an elevation.

Organize the students into groups of two, (1) a builder and (2) a recorder. The roles are consistent across multiple grade levels. Assign the following responsibilities to the group members.

- Builder:

  ‣ Gathers materials

  ‣ Builds the first version

  ‣ Tests and records results on the EDP poster

- Recorder:

  ‣ Draws two or three ideas on the EDP poster

  ▸ Takes apart the first design and gathers materials for the second design

  ▸ Begins building the second version

- Both:

  ▸ Document the define step in the EDP

  ▸ Identify constraints

  ▸ Follow directions and work together

As in the process for younger students, the roles are balanced so students do not feel that one role is less fair or important than the other. For example, the recorder doesn't only write, and the builder doesn't only build; they take turns. The most significant difference for older students is that they identify the goal of the activity and the constraints. As the teacher, you can identify any number of constraints. Examples include the following.

- Give students a budget and apply prices to their materials. Students are not allowed to go over budget.

- Limit the size of the container.

- Limit the weight.

Before students begin, share their EDP poster for them to fill out. Here, they can fill out each part of the EDP.

- **Define:** The students write and share what they are attempting to do and identify all constraints. This step lets the teacher see that both group members understand the goal.

  Example—Our group needs to create a container that keeps the egg from breaking when we drop it from the ladder. The container must fit inside the provided shoebox.

- **Develop solutions:** The recorder draws the two or three initial ideas. Example drawings appear in figure 4.3 (page 64).

- **Optimize:** The builder records the results of the first test. Then, the group analyzes failure points and collaboratively decides on what to do to improve.

  Example—Our first attempt worked! We have room to add more cotton balls, so we will try that and drop the egg from one step higher.

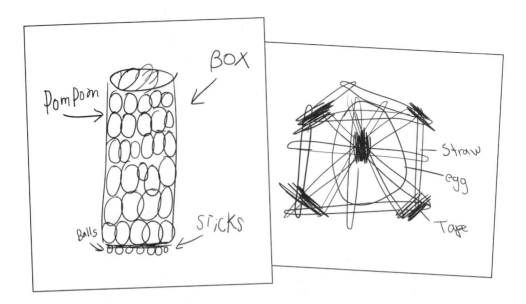

FIGURE 4.3: Two examples of initial design drawings.

Here are some sample student prompts you can provide.

- Can you slow down the descent speed of the egg?
- What is absorbing the impact of the collision instead of the egg?
- Does the orientation of the egg in the container matter?

Again, you should emphasize the lessons learned from multiple iterations, not the height of the egg drop. Have the students comment on how their design changed from their first idea. Ask the students if they had a bold idea. Did it work? Congratulate those students who had an amazing idea and learned from the experience.

What You Can Do Now

Students need to learn that taking risks and failing are OK. Unfortunately, as we saw with the work of Christensen (2016), the best-run companies in the world struggle with embracing failure as an opportunity to learn and innovate. For your classroom, you can reframe STEM lessons so that failure is the goal, you can create a First Penguin Award, you can use the engineering design process, and you can model that making mistakes is OK.

Reframe Your STEM Lessons So Failure Is the Goal

A strategy for teaching students to embrace failure is to make a bulletin board like the one in figure 4.4 at the beginning of the year.

IN OUR CLASSROOM, WE SAY . . .	INSTEAD OF . . .
"We learned these things."	"We failed."
"That was our first attempt."	"We failed."
"We are going to make these changes."	"We failed."
"By observing and listening to the other groups, we have some ideas for improvements."	"We failed."

FIGURE 4.4: Example of a reframe-failure bulletin board.

Create this bulletin board with your students. Make them part of the process to help them understand the message.

Create Your First Penguin Award

Pausch (2008) waited until the end of the semester to give his students the First Penguin Award. You don't need to wait that long. Imparting this award can be a fun activity to do on Friday afternoons. You can also ask students to document their mistakes as an exit ticket (see figure 4.5 for an example) and review students' tickets at the beginning of the next class. Use the exit ticket as an opportunity to reinforce the classroom culture that mistakes and failure are part of the learning process.

Exit Ticket

Name: Jason McKenna

Date: December 29, 2021

My wonderful mistake today: I tried to make my bridge cross three feet, and it wasn't strong enough.

FIGURE 4.5: Example of mistakes as an exit ticket.

Embrace the Engineering Design Process

Can students as young as five or six years old engage in the engineering design process? Yes! They are natural engineers; they love to tinker, play, and explore. Of course, it helps that the EDP makes failure the goal. In addition, the EDP's optimize step reinforces that the first solution is never the correct or final one.

Model That It Is OK to Make Mistakes

Your attitude toward your own mistakes will influence the culture of your classroom. Students will mimic your behavior if you are chagrined when you make a mistake. Share experiences with students when you've learned from failure. Be open to taking chances and trying new things in your classroom. When they don't work, discuss what you learned from the experience. Here are some ideas you can experiment with in your classroom.

GRADES K-2

- Try an interactive bulletin board.

- Create a new learning center.

- Grade and assess. (For more information on grading and assessment, see chapter 6, page 91.)

- Engage with the community to get ideas for school visits and field trips.

- Engage with social media to show off your STEM lessons.

GRADES 3-6

- Use flexible seating.

- Try a new piece of technology.

- Try a new way to engage parents and the community.

- Grade. (For more information on grading and assessment, see chapter 6, page 91.)

- Engage with social media to show off your STEM lessons.

Unfortunately, schools can sometimes lack innovation. Don't be afraid to try new things, learn from mistakes, and share them with your students.

Teacher Spotlight:
Encouraging Students to Take Risks

Jessica deBruyn is a K–8 technology instructor at Sister Thea Bowman Catholic School in Jackson, Mississippi. She has taught STEM to students of different backgrounds and socioeconomic statuses throughout the United States. In the following interview, deBruyn offers her insights into creating a classroom of risk takers (J. deBruyn, personal communication, November 10, 2021).

How do you encourage students to take risks and view failure as an opportunity to learn more?

My classroom instruction is process driven rather than product driven. When students think the product is most important, they tend to see classwork as pass or fail. However, when students think the process is most important, they focus on the journey and growth.

I am also intentional with my vocabulary. I try to avoid saying *right* and *wrong*. Instead, I will say a theory was *proven* or *not proven*, or a system or code *works* or is a *work in progress*.

Another strategy is to model and share personal failures. Students often believe a teacher is an expert who doesn't make mistakes, and they think they are expected to achieve that level of perfection. However, when students see a teacher also makes mistakes, it models that mistakes are acceptable and aren't considered failures.

Sometimes, I intentionally make a mistake on a minor point of instruction. If a student catches my mistake and corrects me, I have created a perfect teachable moment to model how to handle correction. If a student doesn't catch my minor mistake, I can let it go or catch myself a little later in the lesson as I'm reviewing my work. Students need to see that making a mistake does not mean failure and doesn't need to be hidden or cause feelings of embarrassment.

How do you differentiate these techniques from grades K–3 to grades 4–6?

For younger kids, I model intentional failure and use humor. For example, during a STEM lesson using robots in an activity where students tried to push a dragon out of their village, I modeled an incorrect program where the robot missed the dragon completely. However, I used humor instead of getting upset or saying I was wrong. I said, "Oh no, where are you going, robot? He's taking the scenic route to come back around and surprise the dragon."

In the second program I modeled, I had the robot get to the dragon but not push the dragon far enough. I said, "He must be a heavy dragon and need more of a push."

The third program worked, and I celebrated how I learned more about how to give directions to my robot each time.

For students in grades 4–6, I take away the high-stakes stress feeling. Reinforcing for students that the focus is on the process, not the product, helps students feel freer to take risks.

For example, during a computer science lesson, many students created a workable code, but it was not the correct code on the answer key. I told them they did a great job figuring out a process that worked.

continued →

I then challenged them to see if they could find a way to make the process shorter. I gave them hints at first, and when I showed them the answer on the key, I presented it as not the correct answer but simply another way.

When students get down on themselves for failing, what procedures do you employ to change that perception?

I found students face failures in three main ways, each requiring a different procedure.

1. **Failure numbness:** Students feel they have failed their whole lives. Because they feel dumb, they no longer care about the consequences of pass or fail. They will give any response because they are numb to educational feedback.

   With these students, I have found STEM helps mix things up. When they are presented with an open-ended scenario such as building a bridge any way they want that will hold the most pennies, they suddenly can't just write a number or circle an option. They must create something. For example, a competition for the most pennies on the bridge inspires these students, and they respond to the openness of having more than one exactly right answer.

2. **Failure devastation:** Students who are perfectionists experience failure devastation. They tried their best and failed, which they interpret as their best wasn't good enough, so they don't see the point of trying anymore.

   Ironically, partnering these students with a student who is numb to failure is the most successful procedure I've found. The numb student isn't devastated by failing, so they try anything, whether it works or not. By partnering a student who has been devastated by failing with a student who doesn't care about failing, the student fearing failure learns that failing is not so scary.

3. **Failure avoidance:** These kids fear even the idea or potential of failing, so they won't give any answer for fear it will be wrong.

   These are students who will turn in a blank test. They may look like they don't care; however, they care so much they don't want to risk failing, so they will avoid the situation entirely.

   I also pair these students with students who are numb to failing because it teaches them that failing isn't the end of the world, and they slowly begin to decrease their avoidance of giving an answer. In addition, they must participate because their partner is working with them on the project.

Why is it easier to view failure as a learning opportunity in a STEM lesson?

With STEM, there are so many ways to solve a problem. For example, when students don't get the expected answer in a science experiment, they can explain why their results were different, which is still valuable learning. My most successful labs have often been when students' results were unexpected, and we could discuss why. STEM provides the opportunity for open-ended thinking and problem solving, which teaches students that there is not such a black-and-white line for pass or fail.

Describe what you feel are the characteristics of a great STEM lesson.

The greatest STEM lessons I have taught are the simplest. The more complex the lesson, the more convoluted and confusing it is. My guidelines for a great STEM lesson are the following.

- Base it on a real-world problem.
- Include a one-sentence goal.
- Include five or fewer parameters.
- Engage in the EDP.

Key Takeaways

Helping students become risk takers young helps build their confidence throughout their schooling. The following are some key takeaways from this chapter.

- **Cultivate a classroom culture where failure is a goal:** Students will never learn to embrace experimentation and iteration without a supportive classroom culture.

- **Help students internalize that failure is an opportunity to learn:** Also, teach them that if they aren't failing, they aren't innovating.

- **Incentivize failure:** What is the First Penguin Award in your classroom?

- **Use the engineering design process in your STEM lessons:** This process gives students the opportunity to fail and explore multiple solutions to different challenges.

- **Avoid emphasizing a grade:** Once students receive a grade, learning stops. Emphasize the process.

Explore

STEM

Pedagogy

Part 3 focuses on specific guidelines and suggestions for how to teach STEM in your elementary classroom. These chapters will equip you with the context and the specific takeaways to allow you to feel confident about implementing STEM.

CHAPTER 5

Exploring STEM Teaching and Guided Discovery Learning

Memory is the residue of thought.

—Daniel T. Willingham

Nothing is better than seeing a room full of engaged and excited students working in groups to solve a problem. You can hear a certain buzz as you walk into the room. If you teach long enough, you become familiar with that buzz—students are talking but not over one another; students are excited but all on task; students are moving throughout the room but in an organized way.

I visited such a class in the Clark County School District in Nevada. The sixth graders were on a game field, testing their robots in a competition. The student groups each ran their robot, collected a score, and took the robot back to their table to adjust the code, the robot, or both. After each run, students clapped and high-fived one another. Sometimes, a student groaned as a robot didn't complete the last action before time ran out. This wasn't a sporting event—this was STEM.

My favorite part was watching the students discuss what they were going to change before the next run.

- "Let's try changing the velocity of the motor."
- "What if we tried to increase the gear ratio?"

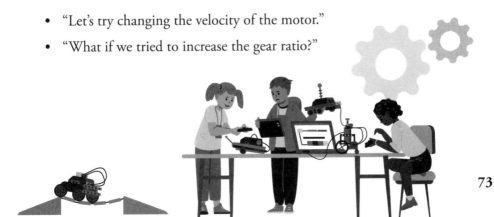

- "I think our strategy is wrong. We pick up all the blue rings before we put any others on a goal."
- "Who should drive first next time?"

Student voice and choice have become popular topics in education (Davis, 2018). In this example, students owned their decisions and were free to make them. In addition, they made decisions collaboratively.

The teacher facilitated. He provided feedback on the students' robot design or code. The teacher encouraged students to look at what the other groups were doing and discuss their projects. Importantly, the teacher was having substantive discussions about different computer science concepts (for example, "I think the sensor is not detecting that object because of your Boolean condition") and engineering concepts (for example, "The arm needs to be extended to reach the highest goal, but is extending the arm going to make your robot tip over?").

These conversations show that students were not simply guessing and checking their way through the challenge. The students and teacher were working from a shared reservoir of knowledge that formed the bulk of their communication. The students knew how to code their robot to make it move and make decisions based on sensor input. And they understood how to build a robot. Now, they were integrating, applying, and extending that knowledge. The students solved problems, collaborated, and iterated using the teacher's guidance. The teacher ensured that the students had the necessary background knowledge in previous lessons to get started. He also ensured that everyone in the class had a shared understanding of success. Finally, he established routines around collaboration, feedback, and iteration.

Unfortunately, the guided discovery learning I saw in Clark County is difficult to accomplish. When observing these classrooms, we teachers might think that we should teach by letting students figure out what to do without any structure. Or, we might think that providing students with structure will stifle their creativity. In this chapter, we explore what the research says about how we can create that classroom buzz of highly motivated and engaged students. We also discuss the knowledge-versus-skills debate, the process of thinking, and the benefits of guided discovery learning.

Understanding Knowledge Versus Skills

Teaching is one of the most challenging jobs in the world. The scope of a teaching job is enormous and often undefined. In addition, there often isn't consensus about teaching priorities. For example, some people say a significant teaching role is to help students learn new concepts and skills, but some push back and say that it is more important for students to learn strategies, not rote memorization.

When I started teaching, I said that I taught students, not subjects. As technology that allows one to instantly search the internet for nearly infinite information became more prevalent, I talked with my colleagues about whether we needed to focus on basic knowledge. I wondered if we should spend time engaging students in activities that promote critical thinking and problem solving, especially considering the students' future careers. The World Economic Forum (2020) published the following list of the top ten job skills needed in 2025 (type of skill is shown in parentheses).

1. Analytical thinking and innovation (problem solving)
2. Active learning and learning strategies (self-management)
3. Complex problem solving (problem solving)
4. Critical thinking and analysis (problem solving)
5. Creativity, originality, and initiative (problem solving)
6. Leadership and social influence (working with people)
7. Technology use, monitoring, and control (technology use and development)
8. Technology design and programming (technology use and development)
9. Resilience, stress tolerance, and flexibility (self-management)
10. Reasoning, problem solving, and ideation (problem solving)

The top ten skills create tension in education about what teachers emphasize to their students. Analytical thinking and innovation? Complex problem solving? Critical thinking and analysis? To teach our students these skills, it makes sense to give them lots of practice in problem solving, critical thinking, innovation, and so on.

However, what is the balance between ensuring students have a reservoir of basic knowledge and facts and ensuring students think critically and problem solve? Is a balance needed? Because students can use tools like the Google search engine to access information, do they need to focus primarily on content? Instead, should students spend most of their time learning skills like problem solving, which they can apply in different contexts? This debate is often referred to as the *knowledge-versus-skills* debate (Sherrington, 2019). The following captures the skills side of this knowledge-versus-skills debate:

> Schools must shift from prioritizing content knowledge to skill development. As long as students are learning to communicate, collaborate and think critically, it doesn't matter what they apply that to. Let them learn about video games, sports or how to make videos on YouTube. As long as they are learning skills it will prove valuable. (Klein, 2020)

The preceding quote assumes that skills are transferable, meaning that once students have learned a skill, it easily transfers to another context. For example, students think critically when learning about video games; therefore, they'll apply those critical-thinking skills when trying to solve a mathematics problem. This misconception about transferring skills is the heart of the knowledge-versus-skills debate. Many teachers believe a tension exists between teaching students content knowledge and teaching them thinking skills (Beghetto, Kaufman, & Baer, 2015).

Mitchel Resnick (2017), professor of learning research at the MIT Media Lab, captures the emphasis on skills over knowledge in his book *Lifelong Kindergarten*. He notes the following:

> The project-based approach takes a broader view of "knowledge." It recognizes that knowledge is not just a collection of concepts. As students work together on projects, they learn not only webs of concepts, but also sets of strategies—strategies for making things, for solving problems, for communicating ideas. (Resnick, 2017, p. 54)

The problem with emphasizing skills is twofold. First, critical thinking and problem solving are not strategies; instead, they are a collection of skills that are difficult to apply generally (Wiliam, 2018b). As teachers, we have seen many students write a paragraph well in language arts class, and then those writing skills don't transfer to history class when the students are asked to write an essay. This exemplifies the difficulty students have with applying their skills to a different context. Second, students need to learn content knowledge to apply the World Economic Forum skills list (page 75). In other words, knowledge precedes skills (Willingham, 2021b).

The emphasis on teaching thinking skills may result from misunderstanding what *thinking* means. Those of us in education have a terrible habit of hand-waving when it comes to terms like this. For example, we say we want our students to become *better thinkers*. No one disagrees with that. But how do we define the criteria for *better thinkers*? We need to do a better job of identifying and examining our terms.

Thinking About Thinking

Many people believe that thinking is a general skill. For example, they expect that students who are great at playing chess should be great at solving problems in mathematics or science class, which is often the rationale used when beginning a chess club. Unfortunately, this is not how thinking works. Thinking is not the same as general skills that can be applied in many contexts (Willingham, 2021b). When Resnick speaks of sets of strategies in the preceding quote, he implies that these strategies can apply to different situations, but research doesn't support that claim (Kirschner & Hendrick, 2020).

What is *thinking* then? To answer that question, let's look at figure 5.1 from Daniel T. Willingham's (2021b) *Why Don't Students Like School? A Cognitive Scientist Answers Questions About How the Mind Works and What It Means for the Classroom.*

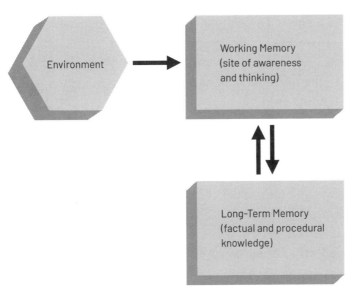

Source: Willingham, 2021b. Copyright © 2021 by Daniel T. Willingham. Used with permission.

FIGURE 5.1: Simplified model of the mind.

First, you take in information from your environment. This includes things that you see, hear, read, and so on. Next, that information goes into your *working memory*. Working memory is the information you are actively and currently thinking about.

For example, imagine Charlie, a fourth-grade student, discovers an unfamiliar word (*vibrate*) while researching ways to make a sound-reducing wall during his STEM class. Charlie rereads the sentence, "When sound waves move through the air, each air molecule vibrates back and forth, hitting the air molecule next to it, which then also vibrates back and forth." Then, Charlie uses context clues to determine the meaning of the unfamiliar word (*vibrate*: to move back and forth). Seeing the word is the information from his environment. When Charlie thinks about the context and understands the word's meaning, he uses his working memory. When he retrieves the meanings of the context clues, those are coming from *long-term memory*.

Another way of thinking of long-term memory is that it contains things you are not constantly conscious of, such as your favorite color, how to make a sandwich, your address, and so on. Things in your long-term memory are not in your immediate awareness.

Let's say I asked you to describe the three steps in the engineering design process (EDP) discussed in chapter 4 (page 55). First, asking the question is part of the environment because you hear the question. Maybe you picture the EDP graphic, or you think about documenting the engineering design process in your engineering notebook. Therefore, you are now actively thinking about the EDP as you answer the question, which is your working memory. You retrieve the information (the memory of the EDP) from your long-term memory. Thus, thinking occurs when you combine information (the question from the environment and the memory of the EDP in your long-term memory) in new ways (Willingham, 2021b). When students are trying to learn something new or solve a problem, they combine information from their environment with information stored in their long-term memory (see figure 5.1, page 77).

The practical application of thinking about thinking to classrooms is this: prior knowledge determines the quality of problem solving. Therefore, experts have more and better prior knowledge than novices do (Kirschner & Hendrick, 2020). Again, the quality of prior knowledge is what makes students better at solving problems—not their application of a general set of strategies.

If prior knowledge is so necessary, how does one acquire it? In other words, how do facts, concepts, or procedures become part of long-term memory? Long-term memory is a product of what one thinks about (Willingham, 2021b). So, if we want elementary and middle school students to remember something, they need to think about it, which may seem obvious, but this has a lot of nuance to it.

As we learned in chapter 2 (page 19) and from Ericsson and Pool's (2016) *Peak*, people's brains are adaptable and capable of learning and doing amazing things. However, Ericsson and Pool (2016) take great pains to emphasize that not just any type of practice is effective. Learning takes proper practice.

Unfortunately, we often work at extremes in education. Tell teachers that students need to build their prior knowledge and engage in deliberate practice as described in *Peak* (Ericsson & Pool, 2016), and many immediately think of drill and kill. Tell teachers not to drill and kill with students, and they leave students to figure everything out on their own. However, we don't need to work in extremes.

Clarifying the Differences Between Unguided and Guided Discovery Learning

Teaching content does not mean we are neglecting the World Economic Forum skills list (page 75). Educational research clearly shows that unguided (or minimally guided) discovery or project-based learning isn't effective (Kirschner & Hendrick, 2020). The easiest way to define unguided discovery learning is to explain what it doesn't have: any direct instruction or delivery of information to foster prior knowledge. However, the quantity and quality of our prior knowledge determine our ability to solve problems.

What happens when students don't have the prior knowledge? What will they do? Going back to *Lifelong Kindergarten*, Resnick (2017) identifies the following as characteristics of good teaching.

- **Catalyst:** Providing a spark (often through questioning) to accelerate the learning process
- **Consultant:** Providing support to students; Resnick (2017) specifically says that consultants should not "deliver instruction" (p. 113).
- **Connector:** Connecting students with peers they can learn from
- **Collaborator:** Creating your own projects and inviting students to join you

So again, the key aspect of unguided discovery learning is the lack of any direct instruction. The emphasis on skills instead of knowledge causes some of this lack. But remember, teaching students *how* to think is most important. You see this in Resnick's (2017) preceding characteristics, which focus on the process of learning, not the transmission of knowledge. However, the problem with that line of thinking is research informs us that the transmission of knowledge is a huge part of learning—it is needed for creativity and critical thinking.

When we see a student engaged in critical thinking, the student is engaged in memory retrieval (Willingham, 2021b). Without the continual transmission of knowledge, that memory retrieval is impossible. For students to make sense of new information, they need to activate their prior knowledge.

The arrows between working memory and long-term memory in figure 5.1 (page 77) move in both directions, illustrating the active engagement of memory retrieval during students' critical thinking. Guided discovery learning is thus effective because it helps students meet two essential criteria for learning (van Kesteren, Krabbendam, & Meeter, 2018).

1. Activating or creating prior knowledge to be used for integrating new knowledge
2. Integrating that prior knowledge into long-term memory

Guided discovery learning takes what we know about how our students learn and provides a framework for classroom implementation. It represents the means to achieve the goals that Resnick (2017) and others communicate. We can have highly engaged classrooms where students have a great deal of ownership, collaborate with each other, and apply creativity while solving problems.

Using Effective Classroom Discussions for Guided Discovery Learning

How can a teacher effectively activate prior knowledge if students are attempting to make sense of different concepts? We want students to have ownership over their learning, but students cannot have total ownership. We have all taught lessons where we ask open-ended questions to create student engagement, and the classroom discussion goes in a hundred different directions. Therefore, let's consider the following example.

When I started teaching robotics to my third-grade students, I planned a lesson for the students to follow simple instructions to construct their robots. The prior knowledge I was attempting to activate was students' following of instructions. So, I began the class with this: "Can any of you tell me about the last time you needed to follow a set of instructions?"

I wanted the students to identify when they had to follow instructions or a process (for example, their morning routine when they arrived at school) and the purpose of those instructions. Then, I planned to talk about the negative consequences for when someone skipped a step in the instructions. Finally, I planned for us to discuss the importance of carefully following the upcoming lesson's build instructions so the robots performed as expected. However, when the first student responded that he must follow the correct instructions when he let his dog outside, that began a flurry of students simultaneously yelling about their pets. I tried to steer the conversation toward following instructions, but the students had utterly lost track of the conversation's original intent.

When young students get enthusiastic about creating a solution to a task, we don't want to dampen that energy. However, we must ensure that whatever students engage in aligns with the lesson's goals. A STEM lesson integrates many concepts, increasing the potential for students to spend effort on concepts outside the lesson's target (Lehrer & Schauble, 2021).

Modeling Effective Classroom Discussions

The preceding experience taught me that teachers must scaffold and model classroom discussions for students to prevent conversations from getting off track.

To scaffold, discuss the expected behaviors in advance of the classroom conversation. Additionally, documenting these behaviors on the whiteboard, a bulletin board, or a classroom poster can act as a helpful reference for students if the behaviors get off track. Finally, model effective classroom discussions and praise students when classroom discussions stay on topic. The following vignette can provide an example.

Mrs. Johnson grabbed her students' attention as they worked in their groups by counting down from five. This procedure allowed students enough time to stop and refocus on her. Because Mrs. Johnson taught second grade, she didn't let the students go long without a check-in; therefore, this procedure happened often.

The students were using the three steps of the EDP to transport animals (table tennis balls or marbles) out of the zoo because of rising floodwaters. Mrs. Johnson had primed the discussion by writing her first question on the board in advance: "So far, what is the most challenging part of your design?" Mrs. Johnson employed a no-hands-up technique in classroom discussions to keep all students engaged. She asked Ahmed to respond first, which he did.

> *"The marbles keep falling off the side of the ramp we are creating."*

> *"OK, that is a great point, Ahmed. Thank you," Mrs. Johnson said. "Let's see if there is anything we can share with Ahmed and his group to help. Maria, I noticed your marbles were not falling off the ramp you created. What did you do?"*

> *"We used clay to build small walls on each side. The walls kept the marbles from rolling out," Maria replied.*

> *"Great idea," Mrs. Johnson said.*

Mrs. Johnson's discussion was effective because it was short and targeted. Providing students with the question ahead of the discussion helped the students stay on task. Also, Mrs. Johnson could use her observation to frame the discussion. For example, she knew Ahmed's group's problem and which group to call on for the answer. Additionally, she had established procedures such as the countdown and no hands up to keep the class running smoothly.

Mrs. Johnson's techniques worked because she used guided discovery learning (not unguided). She provided students with ownership over their learning and promoted active learning while using the students' cognitive architecture to support their learning.

The preceding example shows an effective classroom discussion. The following are some grade-appropriate guidelines for these discussions in grades K–2.

- Use a turn-and-talk strategy.

- Have designated partners so students don't have to find a partner.

- Have a consistent time so students know how long they will discuss.

And these are some grade-appropriate guidelines for discussions in grades 3–6.

- Identify a clear outcome for the discussion.

- Make a collaborative list of characteristics of an effective discussion. Post the list in the classroom.

Implementing Guided Discovery Learning

There are four steps for implementing guided discovery learning. Note that you can perform the first two steps in either order. For example, you can activate prior knowledge and then create a shared goal. You can also begin by creating a shared goal to get students excited and then activate prior knowledge.

1. **Create a shared goal:** For students to solve an open-ended task, the teacher and students must be like-minded on how to solve the task. When students and teachers begin an activity, teachers and students must be on the same page (Witherspoon, Higashi, Schunn, Baehr, & Shoop, 2018).

   For example, in the lesson that opened this chapter, the students and teacher had a shared understanding of the robotics competition. In addition, the students understood how to start the competition, how to score, and how long they had to run their robots before the competition. However, the teacher didn't teach them how to get the highest score. Instead, he ensured that he and the students shared a goal, which allowed the students to focus on iterating and experimenting.

2. **Activate prior knowledge:** Direct instruction at the outset of an open-ended task foregrounds the skills and concepts needed to solve the task. When we sequence direct instruction correctly, the emphasis is on student understanding, not covering facts or guessing and checking. We can't confuse the goal of having students become critical and creative thinkers and problem solvers with the means of getting there (Wiliam, 2018b).

When activating prior knowledge, the teacher has the job of uncovering incorrect assumptions or knowledge that a student may have. When novice students first encounter a problem, they are not empty vessels (Kirschner & Hendrick, 2020). Instead, the students may have incomplete, incorrect, or insufficient knowledge, so the teacher needs to uncover and correct the incomplete, incorrect, or insufficient knowledge.

In the example at the beginning of the chapter, the students had months of experience with robots. They all had the same base robot; they did not have to decide where or how to begin. A key point is the students could see what their peers did. When a particular group scored high, they shared what they did with the entire class. Sharing experiences allowed the students to add and construct prior knowledge in the context of their classroom competition.

3. **Check for understanding:** Formative assessment embedded throughout the lesson allows the teacher to understand and identify student needs, enables the teacher to differentiate teaching, and creates student self-efficacy. The teacher takes on the role of the facilitator by doing ongoing diagnosis of the students' current level of understanding (Witherspoon et al., 2018). Performing ongoing formative assessment while the students work is critical. Therefore, how can a teacher provide help? We'll go into more detail on that in subsequent chapters.

In the robotics competition example, the students practiced constantly. Each time the students completed a run with their robot, they received feedback from the teacher. Also, watching other students with their robots as a form of modeling allowed students to gauge what they were doing in comparison to their peers.

4. **Allow students to apply what they learned on their own:** The teacher takes away scaffolding at the end of the lesson, allowing students to apply what they have learned to a different context. As the students develop their understanding, you can begin fading out the assistance you provide. This step is crucial because it allows students to generalize their understanding beyond the specifics of the activity (Witherspoon et al., 2018). In other words, transfer enables students to take what they have learned and apply it to different situations and contexts. As we discussed earlier, there is not a general skill. To have students apply their learning in different contexts takes proper lesson planning and pedagogy. Guided discovery learning is one example.

Returning to the robotics competition example, students had a chance to make changes after each run and after they got feedback from their teacher. They did this independently, meaning they owned what they were doing. This ownership led to their motivation. They weren't implementing what the teacher told them to. Instead, they were implementing their ideas. You don't need students to figure it out on their own to foster student motivation.

Some teachers may have successfully used pure discovery learning before. As mentioned in the introduction (page 1), every technique works somewhere. However, my firsthand experience with pure discovery learning has been that it discourages and demotivates students because they have unclear goals or outcomes and don't know where to begin.

What You Can Do Now

Guided discovery learning is an effective way to approach STEM pedagogy. STEM classrooms often feature learning that is active and constructive. Our job as teachers includes ensuring that we create these active and constructive learning environments in a way that doesn't contradict our students' cognitive architecture. When designing or evaluating STEM lessons, use the checklist in figure 5.2.

GUIDED DISCOVERY LEARNING STEPS

☐ Step 1: Create a shared goal.
You and the students have a shared understanding of success.

☐ Step 2: Activate prior knowledge.
You foreground essential knowledge. Sequence the lesson's tasks to become gradually more demanding, moving from guided to independent practice.

☐ Step 3: Check for understanding.
You give students with limited prior knowledge direct instruction.

☐ Step 4: Allow students to apply what they learned on their own.
You give students an opportunity to apply what they have learned on their own.

FIGURE 5.2: Guided discovery learning steps assessment tool for STEM lessons.

*Visit **go.SolutionTree.com/instruction** for a free reproducible version of this figure.*

Evaluate STEM lessons using the guided discovery learning steps in this checklist. The following sections illustrate two examples to help you use the steps for guided discovery in your classroom.

Use Guided Discovery Learning in a First-Grade STEM Lesson

In this example lesson, students explore stable structures by building the tallest freestanding tower possible. The teacher introduces the simplified engineering design process from chapter 4 (page 55), and the students can use whatever classroom materials are available (for example, plastic construction blocks, dry spaghetti, marshmallows, and so on).

- **Activate prior knowledge:** Ask the students, "Have you ever been inside a tall building?" or "Have you ever been to a city where you have seen skyscrapers?" Have pictures of towers and skyscrapers available to show students as you are discussing. Ask students to explain in their own words what allows those structures to stand so tall.

- **Create a shared goal:** Have a prebuilt tower to use for a demo to introduce the build. Review some characteristics of the structure with the students (for example, several connections on the main structure). Show students where they can get their materials to make their structures with their groups. Tell students to write their ideas, successes, and failures in their notebooks while building their towers. Show students an example of what a completed notebook page could look like, such as figure 5.3.

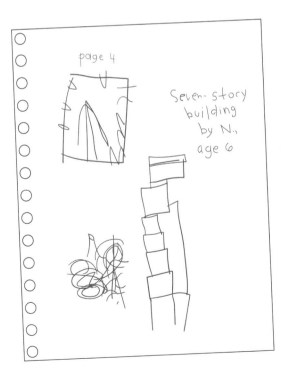

FIGURE 5.3: Sample student notebook page.

- **Check for understanding:** Provide each group of students with a green object, a yellow object, and a red object (for example, cups, erasers, markers, or crayons). Explain the meaning of each color.

  ▶ *Green*—"We are doing great."

  ▶ *Yellow*—"We are unsure of how we are doing."

  ▶ *Red*—"We need help."

  As students build their towers, have them place either the red, yellow, or green object on their desk to represent their current understanding. Then, as you walk around the room, do a brief check-in with each group, and let the object's color lead the discussion (for example, "I see you put a red cup on your desk. What do you need help with?").

- **Allow students to apply what they learned on their own:** Have students improve their tower. After students have built their tower and have seen the other towers, ask students to redesign and rebuild their tower. Ask them to document their ideas in their notebooks.

Use Guided Discovery Learning in a Third-Grade STEM Lesson

In this example lesson, students build and test an inclined plane (see figure 5.4) to examine how these planes change the direction or strength of a force to make work easier.

Source: ©2022 VEX Robotics. Used with permission.

FIGURE 5.4: Sample inclined plane and wheel.

Students will test the lowest of the inclined plane's three height positions, record the distance traveled by a wheel that goes down the plane, and discuss their observations. The students will all combine their data and then draw conclusions as a class. They will use those observations to make predictions and then test the other two heights of the inclined plane.

- **Activate prior knowledge:** Ask the students, "Have you ever gone down a slide? What makes us move down the slide?" Ask students to explain in their own words why people slide down a slide but not down a flat surface like a bench. Give students materials and build instructions to create an inclined plane.

- **Create a shared goal:** Have a prebuilt inclined plane to use for a demo to introduce the build. Show the wheel rolling down the inclined plane at the lowest height.

  Ask students to explain (in their own words) why the wheel behaves differently on a flat plane than on an inclined plane. Then, ask the students to predict how far the wheel will move at the lowest height of their inclined plane and record their findings on their data collection sheet. Show students an example of a completed data collection sheet.

- **Check for understanding:** As soon as every group has made a prediction and measured the wheel's distance traveled at the lowest height of the inclined plane, come together for a brief conversation on the following questions.

  ▶ What data did you collect and why? Consider the purpose of the investigation.

  ▶ Was the actual measurement close to your prediction? What do you think could have made the prediction more accurate?

  ▶ What cause-and-effect relationship did you notice as you rolled the wheel down the inclined plane?

  ▶ How do you think changing the inclined plane's height will affect the distance the wheel travels?

- **Allow students to apply what they learned on their own:** On their data collection sheet, students make and record predictions of how far the wheel will roll at the second and third heights of the inclined plane. They make the predictions based on their observation of how far the wheel traveled at its lowest height. Students should explain their predictions.

Teacher Spotlight:
Helping Teachers Incorporate STEM

Robert Kartychak is an administrator in the Hopewell Area School District of Pennsylvania. In the following interview, Kartychak offers his insights about how administrators can support STEM teachers, especially those using guided discovery learning (R. Kartychak, personal communication, December 20, 2021).

The research states that having a clear shared goal for a project-based STEM lesson is critical for success. How do you help teachers who may want to be entirely inquiry based understand the importance of creating a shared goal with their students?

I acknowledge the value of the inquiry-based method. I foster a discussion with those teachers to determine if their goal is the process or the final product. Additionally, I focus on having a clear and shared goal that helps students achieve a deeper conceptual understanding.

The teacher feedback process is another integral piece for clear and shared goals. Rather than being completely inquiry based, open-ended or reflective questions can be asked through frequent check-ins or informal assessments. Therefore, students can decide if they have considered all options or potentially decide on a different iteration based on the teacher's feedback.

The research states that creating project-based lessons with multiple check-ins (formative assessments) is critical. So, how do you help teachers implement formative assessment?

Using formative assessments is a significant change to educators' mindsets because they are transitioning from assessing learning to assessing the learning process. Therefore, educators need to embrace short formative assessments during project-based lessons to inform the effectiveness of their instruction.

I think you need to start small and gauge how teachers are assessing their students and to what frequency. Depending on where the educator is, I could drill down to a daily exit ticket or some version of a morning meeting where you verbally ask students about their thought process with open-ended questions to grasp their takeaway better. Then, based on the student's understanding, the teacher could provide descriptive feedback to have the student internalize the feedback and determine the next steps without telling the student how they should proceed. Teachers need to ensure frequent assessment, so if there is a student misconception, they can rectify it before it becomes internalized in the student's long-term memory.

Along those same lines, how do you encourage teachers to avoid minimally guided instruction when implementing project-based learning?

I think we make a mistake when we tell teachers that some structure is needed within project-based learning but don't follow that statement with any practical advice or techniques. I think the more specific we can be with teachers, the better. Once teachers become more comfortable, they'll tailor instruction to the needs of their students. But we need to get teachers comfortable first. Guided discovery learning is a great way to provide teachers structure that doesn't stifle creativity and student autonomy.

Why do you feel it is essential to introduce STEM to K–6 students?

The whole notion of traditional schooling is building upon prior years, knowledge, or learning experiences, which is the case for STEM education because children need that experience at a young age. In my experience, elementary students are more inclined to be more divergent thinkers and are less restricted to working in a traditional school framework. Moreover, they are traditionally more persistent and comfortable with needing multiple iterations to solve a problem. This age group is still in Piaget's concrete-operational stage, where educators should harness the start of that logical yet concrete thought process (Börnert-Ringleb & Wilbert, 2018). Waiting until students are in middle school to introduce STEM would be a complete disservice.

How do you deal with students who may have a negative attitude ("I can't do this") toward open-ended STEM lessons?

The essential element for any learning experience is various entry points. At the onset of the task, students lacking confidence could be overwhelmed by the complexity, which solidifies the need for multiple entry points. There should be an entry point that allows a learner at any ability level to have a starting point, get hooked on the content, and want to complete the task successfully.

If a task involves a group, the educator must be deliberate when placing the student with a negative attitude. The group needs to offset potential negativity and be aware of the skills the individual brings to the group.

As an administrator, how have you helped teachers who may be reluctant to use STEM in their classrooms?

Educators I work with initially viewed STEM as something additional to their workload versus working (or thinking) smarter, not harder. I encouraged teachers to be reflective of their existing instructional practices and determine opportunities that would be advantageous to embed STEM. Another method I encouraged was observing peers

continued →

embedding STEM seamlessly, especially in primary classrooms. I was intentional when I would have an upper elementary teacher observe a primary teacher embedding STEM so they would realize that if these experiences occur in kindergarten or first grade, they can occur in fourth or fifth grade.

Teachers are busy and can sometimes have difficulty keeping up with research. What advice would you give to teachers who want to stay current with research? Also, what do you do as an administrator to help?

I want to build capacity in my staff. I'm also aware of teachers' difficulty in keeping up with the research. I encourage them to be active on Twitter or LinkedIn, build a professional network, and support a professional learning community within the school building or district. Also, as new research becomes available, I share it with key stakeholders, who know I have vetted it for them. Finally, when I know of professional development opportunities that further teachers' capacity building, I try to give them access to those opportunities.

Key Takeaways

Guided discovery learning is an ideal framework for a STEM classroom. The following are some key takeaways from this chapter.

- **Remember that thinking is not a general skill:** When students learn something new, they combine new information with information from their long-term memory in novel ways.

- **Remember that memory is the residue of thought:** Information is encoded into students' long-term memories when they are actively processing the information.

- **Activate prior knowledge:** Prior knowledge determines the quality of problem solving.

- **Use guided discovery learning:** Guided discovery learning is a framework used to implement STEM pedagogy effectively. Unguided project-based learning isn't effective in achieving student learning gains.

CHAPTER 6

Making Assessment Student Centered in Elementary STEM Classrooms

(A+)

Is this going to be graded?
—Hundreds of students
during my teaching career

Before I started teaching STEM, I taught sixth-grade language arts. I assigned essays and spent hours marking them, writing thoughtful comments, suggestions, and ideas for improvements. It was a waste of time. Most students ignored my comments and immediately went to the last page to see the letter grade. They only cared about the grade. At the time, I blamed the students. Unfortunately, educators often fall into this trap. In addition, I spent no time thinking about the culture I was creating for my students regarding assessments. I also never gave much thought to the purpose and nature of assessment.

Despite countless books, seminars, and professional development sessions to the contrary, most assessment still consists of sit-down, timed, end-of-unit or end-of-activity written tests with no second chances (Dueck, 2014). I started teaching in 1997. A lot has changed since then: tablet computers, SMART Boards, learning management systems, and virtual and distance learning. However, in some districts, the practice of grading has not changed (Feldman, 2019).

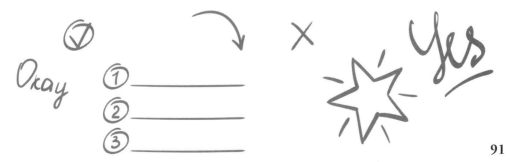

Assessment is important in every subject, but it is even more essential in STEM. As highlighted throughout this book, STEM pedagogy relies on a culture of student collaboration, risk taking, and iteration, as well as creativity, which we will discuss in chapter 7 (page 117). That culture cannot work if the students focus on a grade. To many students, grades communicate finality. In STEM, students are encouraged to iterate, challenge assumptions, and explore different solutions constantly. None of that is compatible with a classroom where students think the only goal is a grade. This chapter defines the purpose of assessment and grading and then discusses making assessment student centered using a five-step process that includes (1) creating clear goals, (2) cocreating learning targets, (3) using ongoing formative assessment, (4) adjusting teaching as needed, and (5) using conversation-based grading.

Defining the Purpose of Assessment and Grading

If our students learned from everything we say or they do, assessment and grading would have no purpose. Grading and assessment are large parts of our teaching. Therefore, it is important that we identify and clarify their purposes.

University of Michigan professor Mark Guzdial (2020a) writes extensively about K–12 computer science education. In the summer of 2020, he wrote a series of blog posts that propose changes to reduce inequity in computer science education. About assessment, he wrote, "What does an *A* mean in your course? The answer likely depends on *why* you teach. Research on teacher beliefs suggests that grading practices are related to teachers' reasons for teaching" (Guzdial, 2020b).

Guzdial's approach to this question as a college professor probably differs from that of many K–6 teachers. In K–6, teaching is anchored by standards. Teachers in districts that still use letter grades usually say an A in their course means students have mastered a subject or concept.

Understanding Assessment

Districts that focus on assessing standards and competencies often use terms like *mastery* and *proficiency* or numerical equivalents of these terms to assist teachers in their assessment. For example, the Next Generation Science Standards (NGSS Lead States, 2013b) have evidence statements (see figure 6.1).

Grade 2: K-PS2-2. Students who demonstrate understanding can: Analyze data to determine if a design solution works as intended to change the speed or direction of an object with a push or a pull.	
Observable features of the student performance by the end of the grade	With guidance, students organize given information using graphical or visual displays (for example, pictures, pictographs, drawings, written observations, tables, charts). The given information students organize includes: • The relative speed or direction of the object before a push or pull is applied (i.e., qualitative measures and expressions of speed and direction; e.g., *faster*, *slower*, descriptions of "which way"). • The relative speed or direction of the object after a push or pull is applied. • How the relative strength of a push or pull affects the speed or direction of an object (i.e., qualitative measures or expressions of strength; e.g., *harder*, *softer*).

Source for standard: NGSS Lead States, 2013b.

FIGURE 6.1: Next Generation Science Standards evidence statements.

Notice how these evidence statements focus on learned skills. At a high level, assessment is either formative or summative. Teachers use formative assessment prescriptively to assess student skill acquisition and better target and differentiate future instruction. True formative assessment never results in a grade. Summative assessment is just that, a summative measure of what a student learned at the end of a unit or school year. Effective STEM instruction relies on formative assessment because, as we discussed in the previous chapter (page 73), checking for understanding is a critical part of guided discovery learning.

Some discussions about assessment focus on validity. Does the test or activity assess what we think it does? Or, perhaps more importantly, does the test accurately reflect what a student has learned? For example, if a third-grade student read at a kindergarten level and then improved their reading comprehension to a second-grade level, does that student get an A? It's a remarkable achievement, but the student is still below grade level. This student would probably struggle with the third-grade standards. If the student does not receive an A, is their grade a true reflection of their progress? Now, we are back to where we started. What does an A mean? And specifically, what does an A mean in STEM content areas?

Understanding Grading

The challenges of grading don't stop with the format an assessment takes. Teachers must also specifically consider what they intend to assess. Let's think more about grading in another example. In a second-grade classroom, students collaborate on a design challenge that investigates different ways to change the speed or direction of an object with a push or pull. At the end of the design challenge, students receive a grade. Let's consider some factors that could impact the grade.

- Students receive points for completing an entry in their engineering notebook daily.

- Students receive points each day for collaborating well with the other students in their group.

- Students receive points for putting their materials away at the end of each class.

Teachers commonly assess all these things when students engage in a STEM activity like the one described here. However, none of these points has anything to do with evidence statements (learning). The preceding list consists of behavior modifications. In other words, teachers incentivize students via a grade to put away their materials or write in their engineering notebooks.

However, does this type of assessment work, and does it reflect the actual purpose of the assessment? What if another second-grade teacher taught the same STEM challenge without any of these elements as part of the grade? Imagine two siblings are in different classes in the same grade. The students each get the same grade for the same assignment, but the grades have different meanings. Is that fair?

When we evaluate students' behavior, we invite a host of problems into our assessment (Feldman, 2019). First, there is the issue of fairness. We discussed the needs of a 21st century, knowledge-based economy in chapter 4 (page 55). So, why do we reward students for behaviors like punctuality and quiet attention as if our students were preparing to work during the Industrial Revolution?

Discussing grading and assessments with teachers can be controversial. As Guzdial's (2020b) quote from earlier shows, assessment practices are often connected to how teachers view their role as educators. Many see grading for behavior as necessary to prepare students for the real world.

When I left education, I quickly learned that my employer didn't highly prize punctuality and quiet. James "Skip" Smith, my first boss after I left the classroom, told me, "We need people to be innovative. That often requires people to be able to work in a collaborative way to solve problems, all while managing risk" (J. Smith, personal communication, November 12, 2021).

As teachers, we often talk about preparing students for the real world, but we don't often have the opportunity to speak to STEM employers. In their 2013 report *Dancing With Robots: Human Skills for Computerized Work*, authors Frank Levy and Richard Murnane reinforce Smith's observations: "The human labor market will center on three kinds of work: solving unstructured problems, working with new information, and carrying out non-routine manual tasks" (p. 3). Smith notes:

> Sometimes, people can think that efficiency is what is important. . . . And yes, we want to get our products to the market quickly so we can capture feedback. But we also need people to take time to understand the "why" and to push on the edges. Challenge assumptions. Find new ways to approach a problem. (J. Smith, personal communication, November 12, 2021)

Smith's comment echoes our discussion in chapter 5 (page 73) about creating a classroom culture where failure is viewed as iteration and a natural step in learning. He describes a workplace and a work culture built on values of trust, iteration, collaboration, and innovation. This work culture echoes the classroom culture we are trying to create with STEM pedagogy. This culture doesn't primarily focus on a grade or grades derived from behaviors like correctly putting a header on a paper.

Therefore, does assigning points to behavior improve student learning and motivation? The research says no (Wiliam, Brookhart, Guskey, & McTighe, 2020). Additionally, our grading practices can condition students to focus on just the grade and not on the learning—this is what leads students to ask, "Is this going to be graded?" or "How many points is this worth?" I've never heard a kindergartner ask those questions, but the questions become more prevalent as students become conditioned to the traditional assessment and grading practices that occur in most elementary schools.

When my colleagues and I discussed grading, the conversations mainly consisted of "Mrs. Miller is an easy grader," or "Mr. Jones grades way too hard." We never had open and honest conversations about the purpose of assessment and grading and how our actions reflected that purpose.

Making Assessment Student Centered

If students (or anyone for that matter) remembered everything teachers said, teaching would be much easier. We wouldn't need to call it *teaching*; it would be called *talking*. Assessment is necessary because we cannot assume students will learn everything we teach. Thus, assessment is the central process of instruction (Wiliam, 2018b).

As Myron Dueck (2021) points out in *Giving Students a Say: Smarter Assessment Practices to Empower and Engage*, the word *assessment* originates from the Latin word *assidere*, which means "to sit beside." Therefore, teachers do student-centered assessment *with* students, sitting beside them. Dueck (2021) writes, "For far too long, assessment is what we have done to students rather than with them" (p. 4).

Incorporating student behavior and real-world preparation into assessments distracts from the goal of student learning. Additionally, we educators sometimes use our teaching or the assessment as the barometer of our success. As educational researcher Dylan Wiliam (2018b) writes in *Embedded Formative Assessment*:

> What sense does it make to talk about a lesson for which the quality of teaching was high but the quality of learning was low? It's rather like a surgeon claiming that an operation was a complete success, but unfortunately, the patient died. (p. 54)

The process of student-centered assessment (as illustrated in figure 6.2) can transform the culture of your classroom. Making students part of the assessment and giving them ownership can eliminate the mindset that causes students to only care about a letter grade or ignore the comments on an essay. The following sections cover each step in this process.

FIGURE 6.2: Process of student-centered assessment.

Create Clear Goals

As discussed in the previous chapter (page 73), students and teachers need to have a shared understanding of success when they are engaging in a project. The rest of the steps in student-centered assessment are impossible to do if clear goals are not established at the outset. Creating clear goals does not mean showing the students the answers. For example, if you are asking students to code a robot so it drives through a maze without touching any of the maze walls, you will first show them a robot going through the maze correctly. Again, this does not mean showing the students the code that you used; instead, it means clearly showing the students the goal of the activity.

Cocreate Learning Targets

The following vignette follows the interaction of a group of students and their teacher as they implemented student-centered assessment in a STEM classroom. Mr. Tran's fifth-grade STEM classroom organizes STEM units around classroom robotics competitions. In this competition, the students would play tug-of-war with their robots. After Tim, Lauren, and Alaina watched a video that showed how the robots would play tug-of-war (creating a shared goal), they began discussing what they would need to do to achieve the highest score possible. Here is the conversation that ensued.

"I think we need to add a gear train to the robot's drivetrain to help increase the robot's power when it is playing tug-of-war," said Tim.

"Yeah, adding gears to the drivetrain and gearing up is a great strategy," said Alaina.

"I think we also need to investigate where to place the rope attachment, the thing that is connecting our robot to our opponent's. We need to make sure we put it somewhere on the robot so if we create all this power with the gear train, it doesn't just pull away from the rope," said Lauren.

Then, Alaina said she could document all the test results with the gear train and the placement of the rope attachment in her engineering notebook. Next, Mr. Tran walked over and began talking to the group.

"OK, where are we with our learning targets?" Mr. Tran asked.

Alaina explained the current thinking of the group. "Hey, Mr. Tran, we think that we will primarily focus on two things while getting our robot ready for tug-of-war. First, we want to create a gear train that gives our robot as much power as possible. Second, we want to experiment with the placement of the rope attachment. When we have this powerful robot, we don't want it to pull away from the rope attachment at the start of a match."

"Sounds like you have a plan so far," Mr. Tran answered. "Have you discussed adding weight to your robot?"

"No," Tim answered. "That's a great idea. If our robot is heavier, it is going to be harder to pull."

"Let's talk about that for a second. Think back to our discussion about forces last week to support your assertion that a heavier robot is going to be harder to pull," said Mr. Tran.

"We discussed that forces, like gravity, always act on objects like our robot. So, when the forces are balanced, the robot won't move," said Lauren.

"That's great. Who can tell me what creates an unbalanced force?" Mr. Tran asked.

"The motors. The motors turn the wheels, which creates an unbalanced force," said Tim.

"Correct. The motor exerts a force onto the shaft, turning the wheel, which creates traction and an unbalanced force. Great answer. However, you still haven't told me why a heavier robot would have an advantage." Mr. Tran added, "Let's include that in our learning targets. Write the targets in your engineering notebooks. Let me chat with another group. Then I'll return, and we can review together."

Mr. Tran then went to another group and had a similar discussion with them. As he did, Tim, Lauren, and Alaina settled on the learning targets pictured in figure 6.3 in their engineering notebooks.

We will be able to:

- Change the location of the rope attachment to make a winning robot in the tug-of-war challenge
- Add a gear train to increase the power of the robot
- Test the robot and write the results in the engineering notebook; next, use the notebook to create an improved robot design
- Figure out why increased weight on the robot will make it harder to pull while playing tug-of-war

---

FIGURE 6.3: Students' chosen learning targets for a STEM lesson.

This example illustrates the first two steps in student-centered assessment: creating a shared goal and then creating learning targets with the students instead of giving them learning objectives written in the language of assessment. For example, percentages, proficiency, and measurable objectives are all the language of assessment. So, why do we teachers use this language with students? And why do we use this language without interaction or collaboration with the students?

Let's get back to Mr. Tran's discussion with his students.

"OK, let's look at the learning targets from your engineering notebooks. Did you come to a consensus?" Mr. Tran asked.

Alaina volunteered and read the learning targets.

"Those sound good. Nice job. I really like how you included the documentation in your engineering notebook," said Mr. Tran. "Let me ask you, how are you competing?"

"Ah, yeah, we need to write that we can identify the rules of the game," said Tim.

"Not just identify, but also apply. It does no good to know the rules and procedures of the competition without applying them correctly," said Mr. Tran.

"Yep, you got it, Mr. Tran," said Lauren.

Mr. Tran identified a gap in the learning targets that the students made. In *Grading Smarter, Not Harder*, Dueck (2014) identifies four categories of learning targets.

1. Knowledge targets ("What do I need to know?")
2. Reasoning targets ("What can I do with what I know?")
3. Skill targets ("What can I demonstrate?")
4. Product targets ("What can I make to show my learning?")

Let's compare the student learning targets in the example with these categories.

- Change the location of the rope attachment to make a winning robot in the tug-of-war challenge. (Skill target: "What can I demonstrate?")
- Add a gear train to increase the power of the robot. (Skill target: "What can I demonstrate?")

- Test the robot and write the results in the engineering notebook. Next, use the notebook to create an improved robot design. (Product targets: "What can I make to show my learning?")

- Figure out why increased weight on the robot will make it harder to pull while playing tug-of-war. (Reasoning target: "What can I do with what I know?")

Mr. Tran noticed the students were missing a knowledge target—understanding and applying the challenge's rules. Mr. Tran also helped the students frame their learning—changing the verb of the learning target to represent a higher-order learning skill. Dueck (2021) refers to this as giving students the "inside scoop" on learning targets (p. 23). Mr. Tran made students part of the assessment process. Students participated in creating learning targets, as opposed to the teacher just sharing learning objectives, and students were discussing those learning targets with the teacher. Students discussed with Mr. Tran the type of learning targets and what those learning targets represented. All of this collaboration is a wonderful example of student-centered assessment.

Use Ongoing Formative Assessment

Formative assessment is the ongoing process of checking for student understanding, and using that information to help guide, or form, instruction to the student.

Returning to Mr. Tran's classroom, let's explore how he involved his students in ongoing formative assessment. He began by initiating a dialogue with Tim, Lauren, and Alaina.

"I see you have a yellow cup on your desk. What's up?"

"We've lost our last four practice matches, and we are not really sure why," Lauren said.

"OK, let's look at your engineering notebook," Mr. Tran said.

The students and teacher collectively looked at the students' engineering notebooks, where they recorded the iterations of the robot, the results of each practice match, and a quick summary of what happened. They also recorded their conversations with the other students, which was required after each match. Finally, the students debriefed, discussing the outcome and the changes they made on their robot, and they recorded their notes in their engineering notebooks. Their engineering notebooks showed a pattern where their robot always had a late start.

The other robots jumped on it immediately, began pulling, and won. Alaina started the discussion.

"I don't get it. Our gear ratio is high. Our robot should be very powerful. So, how are we losing?"

"When we talked to Alex, she said that her group has made their gear ratio smaller, and they are having more success. That doesn't make any sense to me," said Alaina.

"This is a good discussion. Let's think about this for a moment. Previously, we've talked about trade-off. What does that mean?" said Mr. Tran.

"It means when you get better at one thing, you normally lose something somewhere else," said Tim.

"Excellent. With our gear train, what are we sacrificing for more power?" asked Mr. Tran.

"I don't know," said Alaina. Tim and Lauren were not sure either.

"OK, why don't you go chat with Alex? Her group reduced their gear train. Why don't you see what they learned?"

A few minutes later, Lauren returned to Mr. Tran. "We have decided to reduce our gear train. It seems like we are giving up too much speed for the sake of power. We know with our gear train that the wheels will move slowly. We thought that increase in power would work in our favor, but we now realize we need to balance the increase in power with maintaining some speed."

"Great. Make that adjustment, run some more practice matches, and record everything in your engineering notebook," said Mr. Tran.

Mr. Tran's class was now using formative assessment to gauge students' understanding. As was mentioned at the beginning of this section, the assessment drives instruction. In STEM classrooms, where students design and iterate a solution for days or weeks, a teacher must evaluate the students' understanding. This evaluation can form the instruction. We teachers want to take the students' current level of understanding and move it to the desired level (Wiliam, 2018b).

Mr. Tran utilized a popular method of formative assessment where students use three different-colored cups to symbolize their current understanding, as discussed in chapter 5 (page 73).

- **Green:** "We are doing great."

- **Yellow:** "We are unsure of how we are doing."

- **Red:** "We need help."

This way, Mr. Tran could see what his students were communicating. Furthermore, because of how the class was structured, students became instructional resources for one another.

When we think of student collaboration, we often think of students working together. However, when students collaborate by providing explanations and feedback to one another, it can lead to increased learning (Wiliam, 2018b).

The engineering notebooks were also used formatively. Here, the students could engage in a self-assessment. As discussed in chapter 5 (page 73), this can happen only if students have very clear learning goals at the outset. Creating the learning targets with the students makes the learning goals even clearer.

In the preceding example, the students had a plan: increase the torque of their robot with an increased gear ratio and thus win at tug-of-war. Unfortunately, their plan wasn't working, but they were able to use a colored cup to communicate quickly with their teacher. Mr. Tran then used their engineering notebooks to not only check the students' self-assessment but also activate another student as an agent of formative assessment.

The practice rounds that the students did were essentially retesting. When I was teaching, I would have never thought to give a student another chance to take a test. But research clearly shows that students learn more deeply through making mistakes, and testing can be a means to achieve this result (Dueck, 2021). I didn't realize while teaching that we need more testing but less grading (Wiliam, 2018a). Using the three steps of the engineering design process, STEM projects are a perfect way to allow students to think about their mistakes through multiple iterations. At that point, learning depends on the degree to which students believe in their own capacity to learn and improve, which is defined as student *self-efficacy* (DiBenedetto & Schunk, 2022).

Let's take a moment to consider student self-efficacy. Students have two paths to take as they encounter challenges and failures: (1) they can grow, or (2) they can preserve their sense of well-being (Wiliam, 2018b). We often see evidence of the latter when students choose to put little effort into a task and claim the activity was "boring" or "stupid." When students demonstrate the kinds of learning skills detailed throughout this book—risk taking, problem solving, iteration—they show that they believe in their own capacity to grow. They demonstrate self-efficacy. To decide which path to take, students may ask themselves if the task is worth it. Will they be embarrassed if they are wrong? Do they understand what they need to do to succeed?

As teachers, we may feel like an activity is fun or interesting, but more than likely, a student may view participation in that activity as something they have no control over. Research shows that students' self-efficacy, motivation, and belief in their ability to complete their plans decline as they go through school (Wiliam, 2018a). I believe this is because students feel a lessening of ownership over their learning and their capacity to learn as they get older (Anderson et al., 2019). So, how do we help students grow in a positive way?

Let's examine another aspect of Mr. Tran's class. He gave students multiple opportunities to improve their robot's design without penalty. Once again, another opportunity is equivalent to a retest. Most teachers say, "There are no retests in the real world." However, as we have seen throughout this book, many examples of retests exist. Failing fast to learn and being innovative are hallmarks of some of the most successful companies in the world. For example, Amazon updates its online retail site every few seconds (Aijaz, 2019). This rapid iteration gives Amazon the data it needs to determine what works. If people worry about having only one chance to get something right (the current model of assessment in most classrooms), it is challenging to innovate and continuously improve.

When students practice and retest, learning can continue through the grading process. Students gain confidence as each iteration provides them with more information that they are getting closer to the goal, and the collaboration with both their teacher and their peers highly motivates them. Think back to the example of the essay comments that students never read. Learning stops when we add a grade to an activity (Dueck, 2014).

Adjust Teaching as Needed

The purpose of formative assessment is to "form" teaching after we have captured information about student progress via the assessment; assessment drives instruction. We do not need to do this immediately, nor do we need to make the teaching adjustment completely individually. Also, we don't need to have a formal way to adjust the teaching. Mr. Tran used conversation to adjust his teaching. One group of students may need help and guidance on one aspect of the challenge, while another group may need help on something completely different.

The ongoing formative assessment can also help create new learning goals. Not only should assessment drive instruction, but we can also use assessment to adjust learning goals as needed. This process helps both teachers and students develop a deeper understanding of the cocreated learning goals.

Use Conversation-Based Grading

Unfortunately, teachers often feel that a letter grade or a percentage is all that they need to evaluate students at the end of a lesson, activity, or instructional unit. However, the goal here is to make summative assessment more student centered. Research shows that students are remarkable and accurate judges of their work. Therefore, having more opportunities for discussions with students, allowing them to self-report, and giving them a voice in summative assessment can go a long way toward providing accurate and meaningful assessment (Dueck, 2021).

Since students accurately judge their work, it makes sense to converse about it. For example, in *Rebooting Assessment: A Practical Guide for Balancing Conversations, Performances, and Products*, Damian Cooper and Jeff Catania (2022) say:

> As distinct from oral presentations, conversations between students and between students and teachers provide direct insight into students' thinking and depth of understanding. Because conversation is unrehearsed and free-flowing, it provides evidence of critical thinking as students process, analyze, evaluate, and respond to differing points of view, possible approaches and solutions, differing opinions, and competing points of view. The assessor's role is to prompt, listen, respond, and possibly record the conversation. (p. 13)

Unfortunately, many teachers hesitate to use conversation-based grading because our training makes us think that numbers are objective and reliable but words are not. However, think of the field of psychiatry. Psychologists use conversations to treat and understand their patients. In *Projections: A Story of Human Emotions*, Karl Deisseroth (2021), professor of bioengineering, psychiatry, and behavioral sciences at Stanford University, says:

> I had been trained to see brains as biological objects—as they indeed are—organs built from cells and fed by blood. But in psychiatric illness, the organ itself is not damaged in a way we can see, as we can visualize a fractured leg or a weakly pumping heart. It is not the brain's blood supply but rather its hidden communication process, its internal voice, that struggles. There

is nothing we can measure, except with words—the patient's communication, and our own. Psychiatry was organized around the deepest mystery in biology, perhaps in the universe, and I could only use words, my first and greatest passion, to crack open a gate leading to the mystery. (pp. 8–9)

Teachers who are still hesitant to use conversation-based grading could point to the quality of the conversations they are currently having with their students as a reason for their hesitancy. Most parents know the painful experience of asking their child how school was that day and hearing, "I don't know." Although this response is valid, it doesn't reflect the whole picture. So, this is where the cocreation of learning targets plays a role. This can serve as a framework for discussion.

For example, let's use the cocreated learning targets in Mr. Tran's class (see figure 6.4).

Change the location of the rope attachment to make a winning robot in the tug-of-war challenge.
Add a gear train to increase the power of the robot.
Test the robot and write the results in the engineering notebook. Next, use the notebook to create an improved robot design.
Figure out why increased weight on the robot will make it harder to pull while playing tug-of-war.

FIGURE 6.4: Example cocreated learning targets.

Next, Mr. Tran established a scale for the students. It could be something as simple as the chart in figure 6.5 (page 106).

The class needed to establish what *novice*, *apprentice*, and *expert* meant, as in the following example.

- **Expert:** "I feel I fully understand the concept and could teach this to someone else."

- **Apprentice:** "I feel I understand the concept enough to do the competition."

- **Novice:** "I feel I do not understand the concept and do not know how to complete the competition."

LEARNING TARGETS	NOVICE	APPRENTICE	EXPERT
Change the location of the rope attachment to make a winning robot in the tug-of-war challenge.			
Add a gear train to increase the power of the robot.			
Test the robot and write the results in the engineering notebook. Next, use the notebook to create an improved robot design.			
Figure out why increased weight on the robot will make it harder to pull while playing tug-of-war.			

FIGURE 6.5: Example scale for students.

*Visit **go.SolutionTree.com/instruction** for a free reproducible version of this figure.*

The point isn't to create the best rating scale. Instead, the point is to create a scale that the students understand and apply. As seen in figure 6.6, you can add a range to the scale to help with accuracy and reduce ambiguity. Again, we are making students part of the process because assessment should be about learning, not the test. Creating a scale as a class provides insights into students' perceptions and thought processes. Some students may be poor judges of their performances, but this is due to the lack of accurate feedback (Hattie & Yates, 2014).

What if a student wants to inflate their grade? Avoid this problem by having students keep an engineering notebook as part of the engineering design process. In a STEM class, there is evidence in the product because students are designing a solution to an authentic problem or challenge. The product can be the robot, the code, or how the robot performs during the classroom competition. STEM classrooms are full of further evidence of learning.

LEARNING TARGETS	NOVICE		APPRENTICE		EXPERT	
	1	2	1	2	1	2
Change the location of the rope attachment to make a winning robot in the tug-of-war challenge.						
Add a gear train to increase the power of the robot.						
Test the robot and write the results in the engineering notebook. Next, use the notebook to create an improved robot design.						
Figure out why increased weight on the robot will make it harder to pull while playing tug-of-war.						

FIGURE 6.6: Example rating scale.

*Visit **go.SolutionTree.com/instruction** for a free reproducible version of this figure.*

What You Can Do Now

A vital part of making assessment student centered in STEM classrooms is cocreating learning targets. Other strategies for formative assessment include cold calling and the engineering design process. When changing your assessment strategies, be sure to engage other stakeholders in the process. Finally, build a learning profile for your students so they understand and participate in their roles during the assessment process.

Cocreate Learning Targets in Grades K–3

For K–3 students engaged in STEM lessons, we can structure learning targets around three questions.

1. "What problem am I trying to solve?"

2. "What am I making to solve the problem?"

3. "Did what I made work?"

Teachers can add these questions to a document for students. See figure 6.7 for example cocreated learning goals for a STEM challenge on creating a habitat.

STEM CHALLENGE: CREATE A HABITAT!		
Questions	Answers	Cocreated Learning Targets
What problem am I trying to solve?	The animal needs to be in its habitat to survive.	
What am I making to solve the problem?	An animal habitat	
Did what I made work?	Yes!	

FIGURE 6.7: Examples of a second grader's answers to key questions.
*Visit **go.SolutionTree.com/instruction** for a free reproducible version of this figure.*

Students can then work in groups to create the learning targets (see figure 6.8). Encourage students to use both pictures and words.

STEM CHALLENGE: CREATE A HABITAT!		
Questions	Answers	Cocreated Learning Targets
What problem am I trying to solve?	The animal needs to be in its habitat to survive.	I can say what is needed in an animal habitat.
What am I making to solve the problem?	An animal habitat	I can create an animal habitat.
Did what I made work?	Yes!	I can tell my teacher why the habitat is perfect for my animal.

FIGURE 6.8: Examples of second graders' cocreated learning targets.

Use an Engineering Notebook in Grades K–3

For K–3 students, provide more structure by giving them sheets to fill out. Figure 6.9 features an example of an engineering notebook page created for a third-grade student.

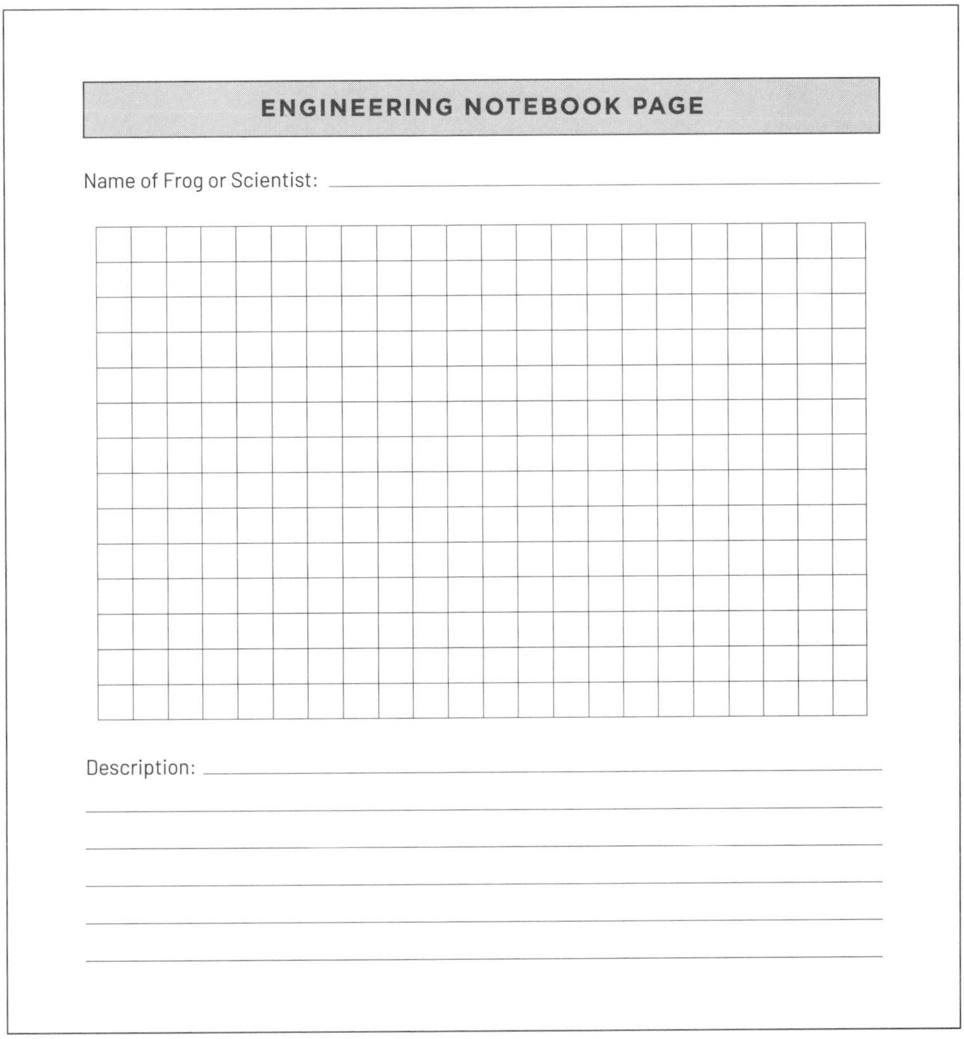

Source: ©2022 VEX Robotics. Used with permission.

FIGURE 6.9: Example engineering notebook page created for a third-grade student.

Visit **go.SolutionTree.com/instruction** for a free reproducible version of this figure.

Next, provide students with samples of what the sheet should look like (such as figure 6.10, page 110). The samples will help create a clear goal for the students.

ENGINEERING NOTEBOOK PAGE

Name of Frog or Scientist: _Tadpole Jerry_

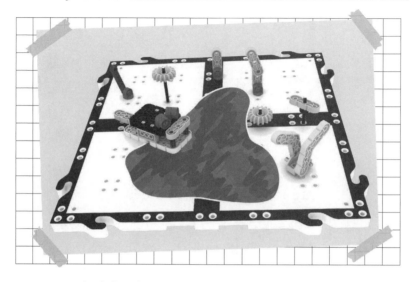

Description: _Whoa! I hatched yesterday! I have so many brothers and sisters,_
some of them haven't hatched. I'm learning to swim, and guess what, I have a
tail! It's kind of weird and my brother says I'm going to grow legs someday.
I can't imagine that. I guess I'm going to adapt so I can go on land sometime.
I wish I could climb a tree.

Source: ©2022 VEX Robotics. Used with permission.

FIGURE 6.10: Example engineering notebook page filled out by a third-grade student.

Use Formative Assessment Strategies

The purpose of formative assessment is to move our students' learning from their current level of understanding to the desired level. Therefore, remember the importance of identifying the desired level of understanding with our students via the cocreation of learning targets. Then, try implementing the following formative assessment strategies.

- **Try cold calling:** The problem with having students raise their hands is that it is difficult to know if the rest of the class understands the material. In *Teach Like a Champion 3.0*, Lemov (2021) says cold calling means no hands up—the teacher can call on any student to answer a question. Cold calling helps keep all students engaged and helps the teacher know if the students understand the material. Some tips on cold calling include the following.

> ▸ Keep it positive. ("Gary, I appreciate the way you look so engaged. Can you identify this gear ratio for me?")
>
> ▸ Make it the norm in your classroom instead of doing it only sometimes.
>
> ▸ Be clear and specific with your questions. (Unspecific: "What does the robot need to do?" Specific: "Who can tell me the first behavior the robot needs to do in our coding project?")
>
> ▸ Ask another question. Return to a student you have recently asked to respond.
>
> ▸ Use wait time. Don't forget to pause when asking a student a question.

- **Embrace the engineering design process:** Students in Mr. Tran's STEM class had multiple opportunities to practice. This practice gives teachers more opportunities for formative assessment. Give students the time and space to go through multiple iterations (the define, develop, and optimize steps) so that other students become instruments of formative assessment. Ask students to share their progress with you, or ask all students to share their progress at the end of class.

- **Use exit tickets:** Students receive exit tickets near the end of class. The exit question should center on a key idea related to an important concept or learning intention. The exit ticket can be as simple as a question on a piece of paper that students turn in as they leave class. Be clear with students that the question isn't graded. Instead, the purpose is to help move the learning forward.

Engage Stakeholders

It's essential not to surprise your administrators with changes to the assessment of your students. Instead, discuss the value of cocreated learning targets based on research, not feelings. Since most administrators work during the summer, that can be an excellent time to engage them in these discussions. The following is an example of a teacher-administrator conversation.

> *"Ms. Rollins, thanks for taking time to chat with me about assessment," said John, a sixth-grade STEM teacher.*

"Absolutely. I appreciate you emailing me the research paper. It was very informative. I try to keep up on these things, but searching for and finding good research is difficult," said Ms. Rollins, who was in her fourth year as head principal at the middle school.

"You're welcome. I thought it could be a good foundation for our conversation. I think the data are clear. Now, I created a unit plan for implementing more student-centered assessments. I think starting with one unit during the first grading period is a good idea. Then, if it goes poorly, I can go back to what I've done before," said John.

"I don't see the risk. Please just keep me updated on how things go," replied Ms. Rollins.

"Will do," said John.

Build a Learning Profile for Your Students

Don't hide that your students are sitting beside you during the assessment process. Communicate to your students early and often what their role is during the assessment process. Building a learning profile with your students helps you remind students that assessment is done with students, not to them. Create a graphic like the one in figure 6.11, and share it with students or post it on a bulletin board.

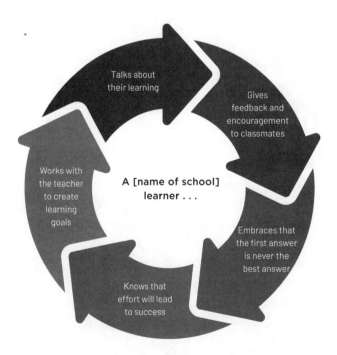

FIGURE 6.11: Example learning profile to share with students.

Teacher Spotlight:
Pursuing Student-Centered Instruction

Myron Dueck (2021) is the author of *Giving Students a Say: Smarter Assessment Practices to Empower and Engage.* He is also vice principal for communicating student learning at School District Number 67 in Penticton, British Columbia, Canada. The following interview with Dueck is based on his experience with student-centered instruction (M. Dueck, personal communication, January 20, 2022).

Many teachers aren't sure how to get started with student-centered instruction. What advice would you provide to those teachers? What is one step they could take to get started with student-centered assessment?

My advice is usually to start small. Create a clear unit plan for your students and have a clear set of objectives. John Hattie says in the foreword of my book to give the students an assessment you already have and ask students to articulate your feedback in their own way. Don't simply tell students to explain their thoughts "in their own words." Instead, ask them to explain the assessment to you just like they were talking with a friend.

In addition, teachers can choose not to focus on the curriculum but engage students in a discussion about their effort and participation. I'm not saying to include that in their grade, but why not report it separately? Have a recording mechanism that articulates effort and participation and have students articulate the amount of effort and participation—not a grade.

In your book, you talk about the elevator pitch. How can teachers give the elevator pitch about student-centered assessment to their administrators?

An elevator pitch must be short. I'd say, "The word *assessment* originates from the Latin *assidere*, meaning 'to sit beside.' For a long time now, we have sat across from our students. I want to roll my chair to the same side of the table to assess my student with them, not to them."

That would be my elevator pitch. If I need to go into more detail, I'd use an analogy. "We are welcoming our students into the cockpit, the learning cockpit. Once we do, should we say to them, 'American Airlines 206 Charlie Bravo on point 9 vector 9 bravo 2 runway 2'? How would they know what that means?"

Let's reconsider our teacher-speak of letter grades and percentages. We don't use that teacher-speak anywhere else.

You want administrators along with you on the journey. I remember sliding a research paper under my principal's door when there was

continued →

a question about something I was doing in my classroom. I found a research article to support what I was doing. He read it and told me to go for it.

You discuss the difference between performance and learning in your book. Can you expand on that?

When reading research from the Bjork Learning and Forgetting Lab at UCLA, I became enthralled with the idea of *performance* versus *learning*. When students work something out, their performance isn't necessarily very high. However, at that moment, their brains are making many connections. So, the performance isn't high, but a lot of cognitive activity (learning) occurs. Now, after repeated practice, students can improve their performance. However, what is interesting is that there is an inverse relationship between performance and learning.

For example, let's say you're teaching adding fractions in fourth-grade mathematics. A student has a question, so you show them how to add the fractions. The student says, "Yes, I got it!" The student has seen it, but did the student learn it? Can the student add fractions a day later? A week later? What if you gave the student a different problem? The performance is high but was there real learning? The research suggests no.

We know creativity is a slow process; however, during that productive struggle, a lot of learning is happening. As you discuss in your book, if we immediately assign a letter grade to that productive struggle, it stops learning and disincentivizes students. Can you expand on that?

One of my favorite keynotes that I give is titled "Failure Is an Option" (a play on the phrase from the movie *Apollo 13*). The keynote's premise is that learning occurs when we position ourselves where we may fail.

For more context, we can examine retrieval versus storage strength. We have two types of storage in our brain—retrieval and storage strength. For example, trying to remember someone's name involves both strengths. You know you remember his name because it is stored, but you can't retrieve it. Here is the connection between performance and learning.

When our retrieval strength is high, we can easily recall something—learning is low. Conversely, when our retrieval strength is low, less learning occurs. So, when a student is performing well, they can quickly recall something; however, that doesn't mean that the student is actively learning. Therefore, how much of the data captured in gradebooks is performance and how much is learning?

Many teachers worry about changing their assessment practices because they feel like grading student behavior and refusing to give students a retest are preparing them for the real world. What are your thoughts on student-centered assessment and the real world?

I have a seventeen-year-old son who owns a business cutting trees and selling firewood. My son talks to customers, deals with problems, meets deadlines, and so on. The real world is teaching my son about the real world. However, I'm not sure if showing up on time for mathematics class is effective for teaching that skill. In other words, reducing a grade for coming late to biology class doesn't prepare that student for the real world.

Furthermore, I think the real world understands standards better than most schools do. When I talk to business owners, I always tell them that teachers say, "If you don't show up on time in the real world, you are going to get fired." Is that true? The business owners say it is complex because finding talent is hard. Additionally, they say that if one of their best employees came in late to work, they would talk to that employee and ask if everything was OK. Then, they would ask how they could help. This answer blows my mind. Why don't we look at how students are doing with the learning targets of the class and then separately look at the soft skills? The real world does that really well.

Key Takeaways

Assessing with students is a powerful tool to increase students' self-efficacy. The following are some key takeaways from this chapter.

- **Consider that assessment can (and should) be student centered:** Assessment should be done with, not to, students.

- **Remember that students don't learn what we teach:** Therefore, assessment is the central process of instruction. Assessment should focus on only learning, not student behavior.

- **Cocreate learning targets with students:** Cocreating learning targets (avoiding the language of assessment) results in student ownership, and students understand the teacher's expectations.

- **Use formative assessment:** Use information gathered during formative assessment to bridge the gap between a student's current understanding and the desired level. Also, use other students as instruments of formative assessment.

- **Use student self-assessment:** Have conversations with your students about their performance. This self-assessment works as an instrument of formative and summative assessment.

CHAPTER 7

Exploring STEM and Creativity

The principal limitation on what creative people can accomplish is what they think they are capable of accomplishing. All students, for example, are potential creators who could experience the joy that results from creating something new. But, first, the students must believe in themselves and their potential.

—Robert J. Sternberg

In 1997, Cheryl Tisch received the antibiotic gentamicin to treat a postoperative infection (Doidge, 2007). Unfortunately, gentamicin can sometimes harm inner ear structures, and her treatment led to the loss of 90 to 95 percent of her vestibular system, which controls balance. Due to her lack of balance, walking without support was difficult. Her vision also was affected.

Fortunately, Paul Bach-y-Rita, a neuroscientist who extensively studied neuroplasticity, used a device (now called the BrainPort Balance Plus) to help Tisch recover. The patient wears a device that sends signals to a metal strip placed under the patient's tongue. The resulting electrotactile stimulation provides the patient with information about head and body position. By wearing this device for increasingly longer durations for a year, Tisch recovered. The device allowed her brain to strengthen and use alternative neural pathways so that Tisch could regain her balance and normal vision.

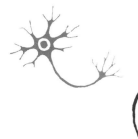
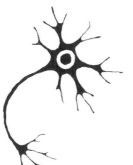
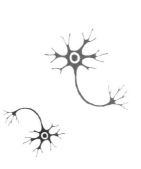

Tisch's story illustrates the concept of *neural plasticity*, the brain's ability to change. Although I didn't refer to it as such, I discussed neural plasticity in chapter 2 (page 19) when I said that our young students don't have mathematics brains or reading brains. Instead, their brains are capable of learning anything. Neural plasticity also applies to creativity. As the quote at the beginning of this chapter states, the principal limitation to students' creativity is their belief in their creative potential. I would take that one step further. We educators have a responsibility to instill in students a belief in their creative potential.

Creative people are not creative because of an inborn trait; rather, they have an attitude toward life that helps them habitually respond to problems in unique ways (Kaufman & Sternberg, 2019). Creativity is a habit. For teachers, this carries implications that they can encourage or discourage (through words or actions) the habit of creativity. Luckily, the concepts discussed in this book, as shown in table 7.1, lend themselves perfectly to the habit of creativity.

Understanding Creativity as a Habit

Before identifying a plan for teaching creativity, let's first discuss the challenges. Creativity researchers Ronald A. Beghetto, James C. Kaufman, and John Baer (2015) identify classroom challenges in *Teaching for Creativity in the Common Core Classroom*.

- Teaching for creativity means educating students to be flexible thinkers within a rigid educational framework.

- Many teachers view teaching for creativity and covering the necessary content as competing, not complementary, goals.

- Teachers never learn how to teach for creativity.

This chapter explains how creativity is a habit that can be formed and how we can teach creativity.

We've talked extensively in this book about not creating a rigid educational framework in your STEM classroom. Chapter 3 (page 37) identified multiple ways to encourage student choice. Chapter 4 (page 55) focused on STEM projects that emphasize student iteration and risk taking. Chapter 6 (page 91) discussed the importance of student-centered assessment. The emphasis on student voice, choice, and open-ended problem solving creates the perfect environment to foster creative thinking.

TABLE 7.1: Procedures for Encouraging the Habit of Creativity in a STEM Classroom

Classroom Procedure That Can Discourage Creativity	Classroom Procedure That Can Encourage Creativity	STEM Connection
Establishing a classroom culture where risk is never rewarded and mistakes are punished	Establishing a classroom culture that encourages risk taking	As discussed in chapter 4 (page 55), open-ended STEM projects are the perfect organizers for creating a classroom culture that embraces risk taking and treats failures as learning opportunities.
Emphasizing letter grades to communicate student learning	Making assessment student centered and providing students with ownership in the assessment process	As discussed in chapter 6 (page 91), STEM lessons provide the perfect context for student-centered assessment.
Emphasizing that there is only one correct answer	Emphasizing and exploring multiple solutions and answers to problems	Using the three steps of the engineering design process (see chapter 4, page 58) during a STEM challenge emphasizes iteration over the identification of one correct answer.
Not placing students in the best position to engage in creative expression	Infusing the classroom with opportunities for student creative expression	As discussed in chapter 5 (page 73), guided discovery learning first establishes a clear goal for the students. Once a clear goal is established, students can work creatively toward a solution.

As a teacher, I viewed teaching creativity and covering content as competing, not complementary, goals. This assumption is almost identical to the one explored in chapter 5 (page 73), where we identified the tension in what teachers should emphasize to their students. We asked, "What is the balance between ensuring students have a reservoir of basic knowledge and facts and ensuring students think critically and problem solve?"

Replace *think critically and problem solve* with *exercise creativity* and we have another question of debate. Fortunately, the answer is the same as in chapter 5: all thinking (creative thinking, innovative thinking, or problem solving) requires content knowledge. In *Teaching for Creativity in the Common Core Classroom*, Beghetto and colleagues (2015) summarize it well: "Creativity researchers and theorists agree that creative achievement—especially creative genius—requires extensive content knowledge" (p. 5).

Acquiring content knowledge does not have to be a passive process. Learning requires students to create meaning and actively and cognitively engage based on prior knowledge. Unfortunately, tension exists between teaching knowledge and teaching creativity. Cognitive scientist Daniel T. Willingham (2021a) summarizes the dilemma in an article titled "How to Foster Creativity in Children":

> The TED Talk with the most views—more than 70 million—is fascinating, inspiring, and wrong. It features the late British educationalist, Ken Robinson, delivering a message that manages to be both grim and uplifting. Grim because he claims that schools are stultifying and kill children's creativity; uplifting because Robinson expresses faith that all children could be brilliant, if adults would just get out of the way.

"Fascinating, inspiring, and wrong." Teaching creativity and teaching content knowledge do not conflict. Therefore, we can view creativity as a habit and explore how to teach and encourage that habit.

Teaching Creativity

Is it possible to know creativity when we see it? Many different opinions exist about what creativity is and how it manifests in a classroom. However, research informs us that people generally believe the following qualities indicate creativity (Beghetto et al., 2015).

- Being willing to do things differently
- Having imagination
- Having unique insight
- Being inquisitive

Teachers can sometimes assume creativity means that there are no wrong answers or students exhibit unconstrained silliness (Beghetto et al., 2015). Although the research doesn't support these assumptions, teachers may pass them on to students.

Creativity has two key components teachers should understand: (1) originality and (2) appropriateness (Beghetto et al., 2015). Most will not be surprised to see that originality is part of creativity. I often hear teachers tell students to think outside the box, which is part of the creative process. The appropriateness aspect is what is interesting, and it blends perfectly into STEM. For example, if I ask students in my third-grade STEM class to create a filter that removes impurities from water, the filter needs to work at some level. This is what it means for the solution to be appropriate.

Notice how this example creates a clear goal (create a filter) and offers a shared understanding of success (the filter must work). We discussed these concepts in chapters 5 (page XX) and 6 (page XX), and now we see them again as measures of appropriateness within creativity. With a good understanding of creativity, we can use that information for teaching creativity in STEM classrooms. Before we discuss the teaching of creativity in more detail, let's identify the different types of creativity we can see in our classrooms.

Understanding Mini-C and Little-C Creativity

Creativity research began in earnest in the 1950s with a focus on two areas: (1) creative genius (for example, Albert Einstein's) and (2) what can be considered everyday creativity (for example, building a drivetrain for a robot; Beghetto, 2018). Research literature for creativity expanded those areas into four. The four C model of creativity presents a developmental trajectory for teachers and schools when faced with hundreds of daily decisions aimed at best teaching creativity (Beghetto et al., 2015).

1. **Mini-C:** Interpretive creativity
2. **Little-C:** Everyday creativity
3. **Pro-C:** Expert creativity
4. **Big-C:** Eminent creativity (genius)

Learning scientists refer to creative genius as *big-C creativity*, while everyday creativity is *little-C creativity*. The distinction between big- and little-C creativity is essential because our students' belief in their ability to be creative is *crucial*. For example, if students think creativity means reaching Einstein levels of genius, then they will have difficulty believing that they can be creative. However, we can emphasize to students that there are different levels of creativity achievable by anyone. Pro-C creativity takes years for students to develop.

Beghetto and colleagues (2015) further this conceptual understanding by helping teachers understand the developmental nature of creativity, revealing insight into the instructional decisions most effective at incorporating and fostering creativity into STEM classrooms. They also state that the intrapersonal nature to create is mini-C creativity, as characterized by the following.

- Have personal insights and interpretations.
- Create personal connections.
- Connect new information to previous learning.

They state little-C creativity is characterized by the following (Beghetto et al., 2015).

- Solve a STEM problem.
- Try different applications for a tool.
- Have unique observations.
- Create an original design or application.

When students combine new information with old information to create meaning, they can create personal insights and reflections—examples of mini-C creativity. A teacher can use feedback and discussions to encourage and expand on mini-C creativity; then students can develop their mini-C ideas into little-C ideas. Tables 7.2 and 7.3 examine the differences between mini- and little-C creativity in elementary STEM classrooms.

As tables 7.2 and 7.3 show, teachers can provide opportunities for students to develop creativity. Furthermore, if teachers and students understand that creativity does not mean students need to reach Shakespearean heights, students can recognize these examples of mini-C creativity as creative acts, which will help students see themselves as being creative. What also helps is when students are willing and emboldened to share their mini-C ideas because the classroom culture encourages student voice and choice and assessment is student centered.

To help us understand how to teach creativity, table 7.4 (page 124) lists specific recommendations from Beghetto and colleagues' (2015) *Teaching for Creativity in the Common Core Classroom*. Also listed is how these recommendations fit with the concepts discussed in this book and with what normally occurs in STEM classrooms. (Chapter 8 has another example of teaching creativity on page 140.)

TABLE 7.2: Mini- and Little-C Creativity in Grades K–2 STEM Classrooms

Activity	Example of Mini-C Creativity	Example of Little-C Creativity
Students create a bridge to span two desks with classroom materials.	Students describe the designs of bridges they have seen in person.	Students use a unique classroom material (for example, a paper towel roll) in their bridge design.
Students create a coding project where their robot uses a sensor to move until it detects an object, then stops.	Students share that the grocery store door automatically opens, which is an example of a sensor in real life.	Student teams create a project that uses a conditional statement inside a loop, thus allowing the robot to avoid multiple objects.
Students collect data about how far an object moves based on the height of an inclined plane.	Students explain the connection between the height of the plane and how far the object moves. The students can use data to support their reasoning.	Students observe that the amount of gravity on the object is unchanged, but the position of the inclined plane can make the object roll farther because of mechanical advantage.

TABLE 7.3: Mini- and Little-C Creativity in Grades 3–6 STEM Classrooms

Activity	Example of Mini-C Creativity	Example of Little-C Creativity
Students compete in an after-school robotics competition.	Student teams take the time to analyze the rules of the competition and devise an initial strategy.	Student teams examine winning robot designs from past competitions and identify what will work well in this year's competition.
Students use dry pasta and glue to create a vehicle for a soapbox derby competition.	Students incorporate what they learned from a previous unit on making stable structures into the creation of their vehicle.	Students incorporate the designs of successful teams that they previously lost to in their vehicle.
Students build and test paper rockets.	Students compare the design of their rocket with rockets from the Apollo missions.	Students create a set of experiments to test different rocket designs and decide on a final design based on data.

TABLE 7.4: Recommendations for Teaching Creativity and Their Applications

Beghetto and Colleagues' (2015) Recommendation	Connection to Previous Chapters	Connection to a STEM Classroom
Set challenging goals.	Chapter 5 (page 73) and chapter 6 (page 91) discuss how to create shared goals in which teachers and students have a clear understanding of success.	STEM learning is an active, constructive process in which students work collaboratively to solve problems.
Encourage students to find personal connections to the activity.	Chapter 3 (page 37) discusses how to help boost buy-in with students.	STEM learning is authentic. It offers learning experiences in which students apply what they are learning in relevant ways.
Minimize the pressure of testing and evaluation.	Chapter 6 (page 91) discusses how to make assessment student centered.	STEM learning emphasizes iteration and collaboration, not evaluation. Evaluation is intrinsic to the goals of the authentic challenge.
Guide students to think of improving their understanding and not focus on task completion.	Chapter 6 (page 91) outlines how to use assessment to guide teaching by eliciting evidence of student learning and understanding.	STEM learning emphasizes creativity, collaboration, and problem solving, not task completion.
Emphasize learning from mistakes.	Chapter 4 (page 55) offers techniques to shift students from thinking about failure to thinking about how failure is an opportunity to learn.	STEM learning features iteration and is an active, constructive process where students are encouraged to make, and learn from, mistakes.

Using the Engineering Design Process to Teach Creativity

Unfortunately, schools often greatly emphasize solving problems but put little emphasis on defining and redefining problems (Kaufman & Sternberg, 2019). Given that defining the problem is the first step of the engineering design process (chapter 4, page 55), how can we help students define and redefine the problem? Figure 7.1 may help; it is inspired by Beghetto's (2018) book *What If? Building Students' Problem-Solving Skills Through Complex Challenges.*

Stop	
Do not move to the next step in the engineering design process until you have answered these questions in your engineering notebook.	
EXPLORE	**PREPARE**
<ul><li>What do I already know?</li><li>What am I being asked to do?</li><li>What are the rules and criteria for solving this challenge?</li><li>What does success in this challenge look like?</li><li>What don't I know about this challenge?</li><li>What is missing from this challenge?</li></ul>	<ul><li>What have I done in the past that will help me with this challenge?</li><li>How can I find more information about this challenge?</li><li>How would I describe the challenge to someone else?</li><li>How can I get help solving this challenge if I get stuck?</li></ul>

Source: Adapted from Beghetto, 2018.

FIGURE 7.1: Thinking about the problem (the define step), grades 3–6.

This approach to thinking about problems can also be adapted for K–2 STEM classrooms (see figure 7.2).

Stop	
Do not move to the next step in the engineering design process until you have answered these questions in your engineering notebook.	
EXPLORE	**PREPARE**
<ul><li>What do I already know?</li><li>What am I being asked to do?</li><li>What are the rules and criteria for solving this challenge?</li><li>What does success in this challenge look like?</li></ul>	<ul><li>How can I find more information about this challenge?</li><li>How can I get help solving this challenge if I get stuck?</li></ul>

Source: Adapted from Beghetto, 2018.

FIGURE 7.2: Thinking about the problem (the define step), grades K–2.

The process of answering the questions in figures 7.1 and 7.2 exemplifies mini-C creativity. Teaching students that these answers are examples of creativity will help students be more creative by fostering self-efficacy and cultivating creativity as a habit of thinking (Kaufman & Sternberg, 2019). Then, in the second and third steps of the engineering design process (develop solutions and optimize), students can develop their mini-C creativity into little-C creativity.

To understand a bit more about how creativity relates to the engineering design process, consider brainstorming. Although it is just one aspect of creativity, people often mistake it for creativity itself. Brainstorming is an example of *divergent thinking*, which occurs in the second step of the engineering design process (develop solutions; Beghetto, 2018). Evaluating ideas, which occurs in the third step (optimize), is an example of *convergent thinking*. However, brainstorming, or any divergent thinking, requires convergent thinking (evaluating ideas) to occur as well, or else it does not help with creativity (Kaufman & Sternberg, 2019). Remember, creativity is both originality and appropriateness. Originality is divergent thinking while consideration of appropriateness is convergent thinking. Both are required for creativity.

What You Can Do Now

For students and teachers, self-efficacy is the most important part of teaching creativity. You can begin by believing that all students can be creative and that you can teach creativity. Also, you can recognize the types of creativity. Students can believe in their creativity by thinking more about a problem before they begin solving it. Additionally, you can invite industry professionals to discuss creativity in their field, and you can model creativity for your students.

Believe That All Students Can Be Creative and You Can Teach Creativity

Teachers can take practical steps to improve their creativity and to believe their students can be creative. Table 7.5 features prompts that remind teachers of their creativity in the classroom.

Recognize Different Types of Creativity Exist

Teach students that creativity does not always occur at the genius level. Here are some examples of providing positive support for mini- and little-C creativity.

- "That is a very creative and unique insight! Thank you for sharing."
- "Wow, connecting that concept to your summer vacation is so creative. Thank you!"
- "This group is doing a great job of thinking about the challenge and identifying a plan. Wonderful!"

TABLE 7.5: Examples of Teacher Creativity

CREATIVITY TRAIT	APPLICATION
New information connected to previous learning	Teachers take experiences from previous lessons and apply them when those lessons are retaught. Teachers also apply lessons learned from interactions with students to other students.
Different application of a tool	Teachers think of ways to take items in their classroom or any surrounding environment and turn them into learning opportunities. Teachers turn classroom chores and other activities into ways to engage and motivate their students.
Unique insight	Teachers offer unique insights to provide the necessary adaptations to their students' work and their lessons.

Have Students Think More About a Problem Before Trying to Solve It

You can apply this concept to any STEM (or non-STEM) lesson using the prompts in table 7.5. Defining and redefining a problem is a great way to foster creativity. Students will often want to quickly get to trying their ideas. Therefore, encourage them to spend time thinking about the problem.

Model Creativity for Your Students

Take time to think about problems and share with students your interpretations of problems. Allow time to share creative expressions. For example, talk through figure 7.1 (page 125) or figure 7.2 (page 125) with your students. Discuss your thoughts and ideas, and then have the students engage in groups.

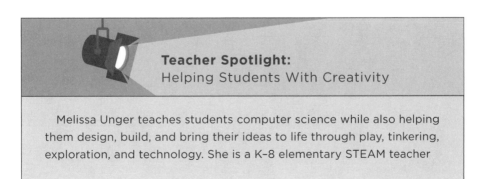

Teacher Spotlight:
Helping Students With Creativity

Melissa Unger teaches students computer science while also helping them design, build, and bring their ideas to life through play, tinkering, exploration, and technology. She is a K–8 elementary STEAM teacher

continued →

in South Fayette School District in McDonald, Pennsylvania. She also leads STEAM professional development for teachers and is coauthor (with Anna V. Blake) of *Capturing Creativity: 20 Easy Ways to Bring Low-Tech STEAM Into Your Classroom* (Unger & Blake, 2021). In the following interview, Unger explains her strategies for teaching creativity in a STEM classroom (M. Unger, personal communication, December 1, 2021).

Why do you feel it is important to introduce STEM and creativity to K–6 students?

Students need ample opportunities to be creative and experiment with their ideas. Unfortunately, the school curriculum is packed, so there is often not much time to add extra things. However, seeing creativity as extra does students a big disservice. There are many studies about creativity in students and adults, and we know that many people lose their sense of creativity as they age. This loss of creativity is a problem because our world relies on creativity and creative solutions to advance and solve problems. By starting early and emphasizing the need for STEM and creativity with our youngest students, we are helping to develop a foundation that will hopefully lead these students to keep their sense of creativity as they age.

How do you deal with students who may have a negative attitude ("I can't do this") toward creativity?

In my experience, many students who display a negative attitude toward creativity lack confidence in their skills. They may feel uncomfortable because they don't know what to do or feel they might do something wrong. I try to instill in my students that it is OK to fail. They might not come to the "correct" answer immediately, or there might not be one correct answer. I try to show students that there are multiple ways to solve a problem and encourage them to try out their own ideas. I also create open-ended design challenges for students to help them develop a greater sense of agency over their work.

What are some simple steps that teachers can take to infuse more creativity into their teaching?

When I feel like my classroom lacks creativity or that students don't have enough chances to express themselves, I pose a problem or challenge and ask them to come up with a way to solve it. Instead of us all working together to solve the problem in the same way, I put students into small groups and allow them time to go about the task in their own way. I am there to guide and support them, but I make sure that I enable them to try their ideas, not necessarily mine.

I also like to give my students simple, open-ended challenges: build the tallest possible tower using three sheets of paper, make a paper chain that is *x* feet long, and so on. These are not necessarily activities connected to the curriculum, but instead are just activities that get students thinking creatively, interacting with each other, and trying something new.

Describe what you feel are the characteristics of a great creativity lesson.

The lesson is presented clearly to students, but the product is open-ended (meaning not all students will make, create, or do the same thing).

Students are given the flexibility to design their own ideas. They brainstorm, gather materials, try out their plan, and have enough time to restart or fix their work if necessary.

Students share their work with others. I think it is essential for students to see other students' creative ideas. Students need to see different ways in which their peers approach a problem to show students that often more than one way exists to do something and to help them gain ideas and grow their own creativity.

What techniques do you use to encourage students to take risks and view failure as an opportunity to learn more?

I try to impress upon my students that although class might be over, or we might have moved on to a different unit, they're never really done with a project. Instead, they can always return to it when inspiration strikes or when they have more information, and improve on their previous work. At the conclusion of class, I often ask students to reflect on different choices they would have made if they had more time or what they would like to change or add to their work.

Additionally, I use a lot of children's literature and the Sixteen Habits of Mind (Costa & Kallick, 2008) to help encourage a growth mindset and help students see themselves as learners. The Sixteen Habits of Mind discuss the nonacademic skills (for example, perseverance) needed for success in school.

Why do you love teaching STEM and creativity?

When designing my lessons, I think about what I would have liked to have learned or experimented with as a student. I also think about how I want students to experience the content: hands-on projects, group activities, and technology tools. Teaching STEM and creativity has so much flexibility because every topic is somehow connected to STEM, creativity, or both. Teaching these topics opens my students' minds to new possibilities and helps them make deeper connections to the world around them, which is so powerful.

Key Takeaways

Helping young students believe in their ability to be creative can help them throughout their lives. The following are some key takeaways from this chapter.

- **Remember that all students can be creative:** Also, students' belief in their ability to be creative is the most important part of teaching creativity.

- **Remember that different types of creativity exist:** These include everyday creativity that we can identify and foster in students.

- **Remember that teaching content knowledge and teaching creativity complement each other:** Teachers shouldn't have to find time to teach creativity.

- **Use STEM challenges to organize teaching creativity:** Students' spending time defining and redefining problems is a key element of creative thought.

CHAPTER 8

Bringing It All Together

It turns out that it doesn't matter very much which school you go to, but it matters very much which classrooms in that school you are in. And it's not class size that makes the difference, nor is it the presence or absence of setting by ability—these have only marginal effects. The only thing that really matters is the quality of the teacher.

—Dylan Wiliam

This book has discussed how to organize and sequence STEM learning, incorporate formative assessment, make assessment student centered, and allow for creativity, and what to say while young students learn. This chapter brings together all these techniques with a series of vignettes that show the big ideas in practice, and it gives examples of what to do when even the most expertly crafted lesson goes wrong. The chapter includes vignettes for different grade levels that illustrate techniques such as organizing STEM learning, ensuring group work works, creating a classroom culture where failure is OK, being creative, working collaboratively, and making choices. Each vignette also contains key takeaways for teachers that summarize the concepts presented. In addition, there is a section that addresses how to organize STEM lessons when teaching across grades K–6. Finally, the chapter ends with a discussion of how to get started with STEM in your classroom.

Organizing STEM Learning While Building a Tower

The Next Generation Science Standards state that engineering design in early grades lets students use tools and materials to solve problems and compare different solutions to determine which one is best. This vignette illustrates these aspects of the engineering design process in action.

131

Students in Mrs. Alsander's kindergarten class were working on the develop-solutions step of the engineering design process. Mrs. Alsander always used cues to remind the students of which step in the engineering design process they were on. The green cup at each group's workstation and the certain piece of music softly playing in the background gave the students visual and auditory cues that they were working on the develop-solutions step.

Mrs. Alsander approached one group of students working on building the tallest tower possible with marshmallows and toothpicks. Samantha was attaching individual toothpicks to marshmallows and giving them to Irina, who was attaching them to the tower. Joey used the sketch they had made during the define step of the engineering design process to guide the build of the tower. Joey also was in charge of testing. After someone added a toothpick, he would count to ten out loud to make sure the structure was still standing for the count. The lesson's goal was to build a tower with five toothpicks. The number five was on the projector as a reminder.

"You seem to be doing very well," said Mrs. Alsander. "Let's share." The students put the materials down and sat attentively.

"How many toothpicks have you used, Irina?" asked Mrs. Alsander.

"Three," Irina said.

"Terrific," Mrs. Alsander said, and the group did a slow, soft clap. "How many toothpicks do we have left to add, Samantha?"

"One more," responded Samantha.

"Thank you, Samantha. I think your answer is about half-right. That's OK! We'll look at it together. I have these five toothpicks." Mrs. Alsander showed the five toothpicks in her hand. "Now, you have used three, so I will place them over here. Samantha, how many do I have left in my hand?"

"Two," said Samantha.

"That's right! Terrific work. That is the number of toothpicks that you still need to add. Everyone, show me with your hands how many toothpicks we need to add," Mrs. Alsander said.

Irina and Samantha showed two fingers. Joey showed one finger.

"Joey, look at the others," said Mrs. Alsander.

Joey held up two fingers.

"Joey, how many more toothpicks do we need?"

"Two," answered Joey.

"Terrific. Now go back and collaborate," said Mrs. Alsander.

Key Takeaways

In this vignette, Mrs. Alsander used a variety of ways to help her students stay on task. The following are some key takeaways.

- **Ensure students and teachers have the same understanding of the activity's goal:** For example, Mrs. Alsander had the number five prominently displayed in the front of the classroom to ensure the students knew they were to use five toothpicks in their tower.

- **Ensure students are all working on the same step:** With students this young, facilitating student groups can be challenging if they are working on different steps of the engineering design process. Mrs. Alsander used both audio and visual cues to remind the students of the step. She had also anticipated where students might struggle, so she was prepared. For example, she didn't have to ask the students to provide her with toothpicks. As a result, she optimized the learning time.

- **Ensure students know their roles:** Each student in the group had a role; Mrs. Alsander did not expect them to self-organize.

- **Call on students:** Mrs. Alsander didn't randomly ask students to respond. Instead, she called on different students in the group, which helped keep all students on task.

- **Create a culture where mistakes are OK:** When students made a mistake, Mrs. Alsander worked with them to get to the correct answer. The students acknowledged and celebrated the correct answer.

- **Establish classroom procedures that optimize learning time:** For example, Mrs. Alsander asked students to focus, which they knew meant to place their attention on her and each other. Next, she told students to collaborate, which helped them transition back to group work.

Ensuring Group Work Works by Rescuing an Astronaut

One of the Next Generation Science Standards for engineering design is "Develop a simple sketch, drawing, or physical model to illustrate how the shape of an object helps it function as needed to solve a given problem" (K-2-ETS1-2; NGSS Lead States, 2013b). This vignette shows that in action.

Mr. Patel addressed his first-grade class sitting in a circle on the classroom rug. "Class, we are ready to share our solutions to the astronaut rescue challenge. But, before we share, let's review our routine for when a group is presenting."

Mr. Patel held up one finger, and the students responded in unison, "Heads up, eyes locked, ears open."

"Terrific. Let's begin with the Incredibles group."

Luisa, Jim, and Josh presented a drawing of the device they used to rescue the astronaut from the crater.

Luisa began, "The string didn't reach all the way, so we tied it to a spaghetti noodle. Next, we used the spaghetti noodle to lower the string to the astronaut. Then, we attached the astronaut to the string with paper clips. Finally, we lifted the astronaut." The group's classmates clapped their hands to show their approval.

Jim said, "We added paper clips because we couldn't tie the string on the astronaut—it kept falling off." Jim giggled, and the students again clapped their hands.

Finally, Josh added, "Our goal was to create something to solve a problem. We think we did a good job because we rescued the astronaut from the crater. We helped and encouraged each other until we figured out to use the paper clips."

Mr. Patel told the students they did an amazing job. Then, the STEM Stars group shared their results.

Cara began. "We wanted to make a contraption to pull the astronaut up from the crater. We took Tom's round pencil container and taped the string onto one end. Then, we rolled the container to pull up the astronaut." Cara showed the string taped to the pencil container, and the students clapped six times.

"Since we used our tape already, we weren't sure how to attach the string to the astronaut, but we experimented with Play-Doh, and it worked," said Tom.

"Our goal was to experiment until we found a tool to solve a problem. We think we made our goal because we rescued the astronaut," Linda said, followed by the students clapping in approval.

"Great job, STEM Stars," Mr. Patel said. "That is a great device you made with the pencil container. That is called a pulley. *I'll add* pulley *to our STEM word wall this afternoon. It's wonderful that the STEM Stars and the Incredibles created different ways to solve the same problem."*

Key Takeaways

In this vignette, Mr. Patel ensured that the group work worked. The following are some key takeaways.

- **Use names for student groups:** Naming the groups created an identity for each group, built buy-in, and helped with student engagement. It also allowed Mr. Patel to praise the group and the group's work, not each student. This technique helps with student self-efficacy.

- **Value participation:** Mr. Patel created a classroom culture where participation was valued. He began by reminding students how to act when other students were presenting (heads up, eyes locked, ears open). Next, Mr. Patel encouraged students to clap to show they were engaging with the speakers. He limited the number of claps to avoid issues of transition.

- **Collaborate with students on learning targets:** Mr. Patel used an activity with a clear goal (rescue the astronaut figurine from a crater) that had multiple ways to solve the problem. Students made learning targets with Mr. Patel and reported on them. The Next Generation Science Standards for engineering design (NGSS Lead States, 2013b) are as follows:

  > Ask questions, make observations, and gather information about a situation people want to change to define a simple problem that can be solved through the development of a new or improved object or tool. (K-2-ETS1-1)

Develop a simple sketch, drawing, or physical model to illustrate how the shape of an object helps it function as needed to solve a given problem. (K-2-ETS1-2)

Analyze data from tests of two objects designed to solve the same problem to compare the strengths and weaknesses of how each performs. (K-2-ETS1-3)

Mr. Patel could communicate these standards with his students by creating learning targets with them, instead of using the language of the standards. This engaged the students while making the standards more achievable.

- **Assign roles for group work:** One student presented the group's creation, another student presented the group's challenges, and a third student presented the success of reaching the cocreated learning target.

Creating a Classroom Culture Where Failure Is OK by Moving a Mars Rover

The Next Generation Science Standards identify science and engineering practices. One of these practices states, "Scientists and engineers plan and carry out investigations in the field or laboratory, working collaboratively as well as individually. Their investigations are systematic and require clarifying what counts as data and identifying variables or parameters" (NGSS Lead States, 2013b). The following vignette shows students planning and carrying out an investigation.

Ms. Taylor's third-grade students stood around a table with a mat, which served as a replica of Mars's surface. The students were building and coding robots in a challenge designed after the NASA Mars 2020 mission. On Mars, rovers find, collect, and cache geological samples.

Ms. Taylor shared background information about the NASA Mars 2020 mission. Next, she asked students to share what they knew about Mars. She listed those ideas on the board. Then, Ms. Taylor tasked students to build their robot and code it to travel to a spot on the mat to collect geological samples.

Ms. Taylor asked the students what behaviors the robot needed to perform to complete its task.

"What is the first behavior that our robot needs to perform, Carl?" Ms. Taylor asked.

"It needs to drive forward," said Carl.

"You are 50 percent correct. Miguel, what else do we need to include?"

"We need to tell the robot how far to drive forward. It must drive forward twelve inches," said Miguel.

"Yes. Excellent. Carl, what is the first behavior the robot needs to perform?"

"The robot needs to drive forward twelve inches."

"Yes. There was a movie about astronauts that came out many years ago called The Right Stuff *(Kaufman, 1983). A person had to have the right stuff to become an astronaut. Well, I want to let all of you know that each of you has the right stuff to become an astronaut or anything else you want to be."*

Ms. Taylor then directed the students' attention to a bulletin board in the classroom (see figure 8.1).

MS. TAYLOR'S CLASSROOM	
We say . . .	**Instead of . . .**
"I haven't found the answer *yet*." "Can I ask a *question* about it?"	"I don't know."
"I didn't make a mistake. I *learned* something."	"I failed."
"I can do anything if I keep *trying*."	"I'm not good at this."
"I am *excited* to try a new method."	"I'm frustrated that my solution didn't work."

FIGURE 8.1: Ms. Taylor's bulletin board.

Ms. Taylor and her students read each of the *we say* statements together. Next, she organized the students into their groups, where they started on their projects. Later, as students tested their projects, Ms. Taylor walked around the room and checked on their progress. She stopped at one group where a student seemed frustrated.

"Hey, Shelly," said Ms. Taylor. "How is the Mars rover doing?"

"Not so great," said Shelly. "It isn't going to the right place all the time. Sometimes it does, but sometimes it doesn't. We have checked the code. It should work, but it doesn't."

"I understand. You say that you checked the code. Can you try anything else to identify the problem?" said Ms. Taylor.

"Can we demonstrate running the robot?" asked Shelly.

"Sure."

Shelly and her group placed their robot on the table and ran the project. The robot went to the target. They ran the project a second time, and the robot missed its target by a few inches. Ms. Taylor said, "Let me run the project three times. Watch me closely and see if I do anything differently."

Ms. Taylor took the robot and carefully placed it at the front of the table. The robot went to its target. Then, she took the robot and ensured it began in the same spot. She reran the project, and the robot went to the target. She repeated this process a third time with the same result. Finally, Ms. Taylor asked Shelly what made the robot succeed in going to the target.

"You made sure that you started the robot in the same spot each time," said Shelly.

"Yes! That's it. I think you found your issue and learned something through that process. What did you learn?" asked Ms. Taylor.

"We learned to make sure that we start our robot in the same spot every time."

"Yes." Then, Ms. Taylor directed the group to the bulletin board and said, "Great job asking a question and embracing your mistake as a learning opportunity."

Once students completed their initial challenge, they chose a new one from the choice board (see figure 8.2).

MARS ROVER CHOICE BOARD		
Design and build an extension onto your robot to help collect samples. Can you create something to push, pull, or hold the samples as the code returns them to the base?	Imagine a crater between your robot and the first sample. Then, create a project to drive around the obstacle, collect the sample, and return the sample to base.	Use a sensor to find samples no matter where they are on Mars. Can you create one project that will find a sample no matter where it is placed?

FIGURE 8.2: Choice board in Ms. Taylor's class.

Key Takeaways

In this vignette, Ms. Taylor created a classroom culture that let her students know mistakes were OK. The following are some key takeaways.

- **Activate prior knowledge:** Ms. Taylor activated her students' prior knowledge by discussing with them what they had previously learned about Mars. She also activated prior knowledge about the robot behaviors and helped students with incorrect assumptions.

- **Create a culture where mistakes are OK:** When a student answers a question incorrectly, as Carl did in the vignette, teachers will ask another student to respond. However, Ms. Taylor returned to Carl after the correct answer was identified. This technique ensures that the original student has understood their mistake. This action by Ms. Taylor accomplished two goals. First, as discussed in chapter 4 (page 55), it encouraged a classroom culture where students felt comfortable making mistakes. Second, Ms. Taylor's actions showed Carl she cared that he understood. This might not seem like a big deal in an isolated case. However, when done over time, ensuring students know their teacher cares that they understand fosters a classroom culture where every student's learning is valued and every student is expected to learn.

- **Use a no-opt-out procedure:** Unfortunately, "I don't know" is often the default response for many students. Ms. Taylor created procedures in her classroom to address that problem before it occurred. This example of the *no-opt-out procedure* is discussed in chapter 3 (page 37). Instead of telling students they could not say, "I don't know," Ms. Taylor provided alternatives.

- **Use a choice board:** A choice board helps with student engagement and allows students to apply what they have learned on their own. Each activity allows students to generalize their understanding beyond the specifics of the first challenge. As discussed in chapter 3 (page 37), this is a great way for students to demonstrate transfer.

- **Emphasize that all students can be successful:** Ms. Taylor's discussion about the right stuff and the bulletin board in her classroom emphasized all students could be successful. In addition, the classroom culture helped combat any negative stereotypes students could have about their STEM abilities.

Being Creative by Preparing to Design a Crane

Ronald A. Beghetto, author and creativity scholar, has identified that two key components to creativity are originality and appropriateness (Beghetto et al., 2015). Both of those characteristics are shown in the following vignette.

Anil, Sarah, and Kim had various building materials (pieces of wood, string, clips, knobs, and so on) strewn around them. The fifth graders were working on building a crane. The crane had to lift and place objects on two floors of a building. In the middle of the classroom, a narrow bookshelf represented the building. The first two shelves represented the two floors. Students would transport one dry-erase marker onto each floor. A task constraint was that the crane's base could not be larger than a shoebox.

> *"I remember the last time we had a project, we tried to build the entire thing, and that was a mistake," said Anil. "We should probably build the base first and make sure it fits into a shoebox."*

> *"Is there anything else we need to think about, or just that the base has to fit inside of the shoebox?" asked Kim.*

> *"Well, the crane must lift a dry-erase marker and place it on each of the two floors," said Anil.*

> *"So, the bucket of the crane must be able to carry the dry-erase marker, which is long. We need to remember that when making the bucket. It isn't heavy, but the dry-erase marker can't fall off because we won't be able to pick it back up," said Sarah.*

> *"That's great. Let me get the engineering notebook and start writing this down," Kim said. "Last time, my group forgot to do that at the beginning of the project, and we forgot a lot of these things when we*

started building." The group members spent a few minutes documenting items in their engineering notebook.

"Also, looking at the build instructions, they don't say that the crane must be motorized. That means that we can operate the string on the arm of the crane," said Anil.

"Good point. So, we need to crank the string to pull something up. It reminds me of fishing. The arm of the crane is the pole, and then we reel up the dry-erase marker just like we would a fish," said Sarah.

"Wow, that is a great idea. We have thread in the material box. That will be perfect to use because it is thin like a fishing line. We don't need the string to be thick since the markers aren't heavy," said Kim.

"And we can use a design just like a fishing pole. Just put the thread through holes on a pole. One thing I'm still thinking about is how we can crank the string. What is going to be the reel?" Anil asked.

"Hmm, I haven't thought of that yet either," Kim said. The students thought for a few moments before Kim added, "Why don't we talk to some of the other groups and see what they are doing?"

"That's a great idea. Why don't we test ideas from the other groups and then decide which one we like the best?" said Sarah.

Anil and Kim agreed. Then, Anil documented their idea for the arm in the group's engineering notebook while Sarah and Kim talked to the other groups.

This vignette offers the opportunity to break down teaching creativity as discussed in chapter 7 (page 117). Table 8.1 features recommendations for teaching creativity and defines their applications in the preceding vignette.

TABLE 8.1: Creativity Applications

Recommendation for Teaching Creativity	Application in the Vignette
Set challenging goals.	The students were tasked with using different materials in the room to build a crane. The task also had constraints: the base of the crane had to be a certain size, and the crane had to complete two tasks.

continued →

Encourage students to find personal connections to the activity.	The students connected the design of the crane with a fishing rod.
Minimize the pressure of testing and evaluation.	Throughout the vignette, the students were not rushed due to time or testing. The students were taking time to document their ideas and test multiple ideas.
Guide students to think of improving their understanding and not focus on task completion.	The students focused on coming up with ideas and thinking, not on trying to get an answer as quickly as possible.
Emphasize learning from mistakes.	The students referenced past mistakes and implemented what they had learned as a result of those mistakes.

The vignette also shows different *types* of creativity (see table 8.2) as discussed in chapter 7 (page 117).

TABLE 8.2: Examples of Creativity Types

Example of Mini-C Creativity	Example of Little-C Creativity
Students took time to analyze the rules and constraints of their crane challenge. Students were also thinking of and evaluating different design ideas.	Students looked at what other students in their class were using for their crane and then determined how they could apply those ideas to their crane.
Students discussed different methods to build their crane.	Students tested different cranks to build their crane.
Students identified that they didn't need a thick string to pick up the dry-erase markers.	Students collaboratively decided to use thread for their crane based on the unique connection they made between a crane and a fishing rod.

Key Takeaways

In this vignette, a group of students used the engineering design process to create a unique solution to a problem. The following are some key takeaways.

- **Remember that a STEM activity is an opportunity for teaching creativity:** The vignette is a great example of a STEM activity that is infused with creativity. Chapter 7 (page 117) outlines recommendations for teaching creativity. You can see each of those recommendations at work in table 8.1 (page 141).

- **Remember that the engineering design process is a great way to organize creative problem solving:** The vignette shows students using mistakes as feedback, documenting their learning, and learning from their peers.

Making Choices and Collaborating in a Robotics Competition

Mrs. Chang, a sixth-grade science teacher, was volunteering at a local school's robotics competition. She always enjoyed volunteering as a judge for local science fairs. Mrs. Chang didn't know a lot about robots, but she loved judging robotics competitions because of the enthusiasm of the students. She loved seeing the students interacting so well together—she especially got a kick out of seeing students on a team wearing team shirts and sometimes even costumes. Mrs. Chang was just getting started interviewing her first team of sixth graders at the robotics competition.

"OK, let's get started. Why don't you tell me about your robot?" Mrs. Chang asked.

One student answered, "Our robot has a basic four-wheel drive-train. People have told us that our robot looks complicated. It isn't. It is just a basic drivetrain and an intake."

Another student said, "We have a frame around the drivetrain to make sure the beanbags don't come out once we collect them. That's why people think it is complicated."

The first student continued, "We didn't want to include too much because when we did that before, we ran into coding issues. We wanted to make sure that we could build something that we could code."

"I see the intake mechanism that you have there. Was this your first idea for an intake, or did you go through different ideas?" Mrs. Chang asked.

"The mechanism was my idea!" a student said. "We all researched different parts of the robot. Intake mechanisms were my job."

Mrs. Chang smiled and asked, "How did you do your research?"

"Mostly YouTube. The competition from a few years ago had a similar challenge, so I watched matches from that year and looked at their intake mechanisms," said another student.

"Wow, that is impressive. Would someone like to tell me about your game strategy?"

"This game is so fun because you can collect the beanbags and drop them off on certain parts of the field based on their color. Our strategy was all about trying to get the most beanbags within the time limit. Blue beanbags get you a higher score, but we decided to collect more beanbags instead of just getting the ones with the highest point value."

"How did you decide on this strategy? What happens when someone has a different strategy?" Mrs. Chang asked.

"We use data to decide. We analyze the rules and then test each strategy as if we had a perfect robot. That is the first test. Then, we list what we need for each strategy. Then, we compare that list to our team's strengths. That is the first thing we do; we list our strengths." One student pulled out their engineering notebook and showed their list.

"I see that you have listed driving the robot is your biggest weakness. Why?" said Mrs. Chang.

"We just don't have enough time to practice. Because there is only one robot, we just don't have a lot of time to practice our driving skills," said a student.

"So, if a certain strategy requires more complex driving, you take that into consideration?" asked Mrs. Chang. The students nodded. "Thank you for sharing with me. I'm impressed with everything you've had to say. Good luck in today's competition."

Key Takeaways

In this vignette, students could articulate their choices and reasoning for a visitor at a robotics competition. The following are some key takeaways.

- **Give students a choice:** Students were given a choice, and they could articulate their choices during their discussion with Mrs. Chang. As discussed in chapter 3 (page 37), student choice is essential to keep students motivated and engaged.

- **Teach students to make decisions collaboratively:** Students could communicate how they collaboratively made decisions. Students are more likely to take ownership of these decisions when they feel like they have ownership over the entire process.

- **Ensure students understand the goals:** The activity that the students were engaging with (robotics competition) was robust enough to keep all the students engaged. However, the students had access to resources (researching games from previous years) to help them develop their game strategy. The students could communicate the goal of the competition and how to score points. Because the robotics competition had a clear goal, its open-endedness didn't discourage the students.

- **Build belonging:** The students all felt like they were part of a team. This led to high levels of engagement and motivation. More about this topic appears in chapter 3 (page 37).

Teaching STEM Across Grade Bands by Creating a Weather Station

Sometimes, STEM activities are incorporated into a science or mathematics class. Other times, STEM is taught as a stand-alone subject. With the latter, a STEM teacher often teaches STEM across multiple grades. Mr. Collins, a K–6 STEM teacher, had his students in grades K–6 create a weather station. He made a chart (see figure 8.3) to show how the activity progressed from grade to grade.

WEATHER STATION ACTIVITY	
Grade Band	**Activity**
K–2	Students will create a weather station with a rain gauge and thermometer. Using those tools, students will log their own observations in their data collection sheets and then communicate any patterns they see.
3–4	Students will extend their weather station by creating and adding a wind vane. They will also extend their data collection sheets by adding tables and graphs to support the analysis they create.
5–6	Students will further extend their weather station by creating and adding a barometer. They will also extend their data collection sheets by adding tables and graphs to support the analysis they create. Students will collect information each morning and record themselves doing a daily weather forecast.

FIGURE 8.3: Mr. Collins's weather station activity.

Because Mr. Collins was teaching STEM classes from kindergarten to grade 6, he used a list (see figure 8.4) to ensure each of his lessons followed good lesson design and presented STEM in an integrated fashion.

WHAT EACH LESSON INCLUDES	GRADE BAND	EVIDENCE	INTEGRATED STEM
A Clear Goal	K–2	The lesson goal is on a bulletin board that we read together at the beginning of each class.	Science— studying weather Mathematics—identifying and communicating patterns; analyzing data Engineering—creating a weather station device
	3–4	Students use an exit ticket to write the goal of the lesson.	
	5–6	Students use an exit ticket to write the goal of the lesson.	
Multiple Opportunities to Check for Understanding	K–2	Data collection sheets are marked with a check mark where students are prompted to show work.	
	3–4	Students check in after each device is built. Data collection sheets are marked with a check mark where students are prompted to show work.	
	5–6	Students check in after each device is built. Data collection sheets are marked with a check mark where students are prompted to show work.	

A Variety of Approaches to Engage Students	K–2	Students are engaged in writing, measurement, observation, hands-on, and collaborative approaches.	
	3–4	Students are engaged in writing, measurement, observation, hands-on, and collaborative approaches.	
	5–6	Students are engaged in writing, measurement, observation, hands-on, and collaborative approaches.	
Opportunities to Apply What Was Learned	K–2	Students identify and communicate weather trends and patterns.	
	3–4	Students identify and communicate weather trends and patterns.	
	5–6	Students make weather predictions.	

FIGURE 8.4: STEM lesson list from Mr. Collins's classes.

*Visit **go.SolutionTree.com/instruction** for a free reproducible version of this figure.*

The students in Mr. Collins's classes had fun creating their weather stations. At the conclusion of the activity, Mr. Collins had each of his classes share their thoughts. Mr. Collins would engage each student in a conversation about the activity. With his younger students, he would engage each group separately while the others engaged in different activities at the learning stations. With his older students, he would move back and forth between the whole group and smaller group discussions. To help guide the discussions, Mr. Collins gave students a framework (see figure 8.5, page 148).

WEATHER STATION ACTIVITY: SHARE	
Grade Band	**Things to Consider**
K–2	What did I add to the data collection sheet? Did I talk about weather patterns with my teacher? How many measurements did I take with the thermometer or rain gauge? I got along well with all my group.
3–4	What did I add to the data collection sheet? How did I help create the tables and graphs that were used? Did I talk about weather patterns with my teacher? How many measurements did I take? How did I help create the weather vane? I shared ideas with my group. I got along well with all my group.
5–6	What did I add to the data collection sheet? How did I help create the weather station? Did I discuss weather predictions, and was I able to support those predictions with evidence? I shared ideas with my group. How did I collaborate with my group to make decisions?

FIGURE 8.5: Weather station activity share prompts.

Mr. Collins was able to scaffold his teaching across multiple grade levels. His younger students could make a weather station while his older students were still challenged enough by the activity. Choosing an activity that could apply to multiple grades allowed Mr. Collins to focus on items like the share prompts instead of creating new activities for different grades. Additionally, Mr. Collins was able to ensure that the activity met the requirements for good lesson design.

Key Takeaways

In this vignette, Mr. Collins was able to structure his STEM activity so that it worked for multiple grade levels. The following are some key takeaways.

- **Choose activities that are easily scaled across multiple grade levels:** This choice cut down on the time Mr. Collins needed to prepare for each class. As a result, he could focus on his teaching (displayed in figure 8.4, page 147) instead of trying to find lessons and activities for his students to complete.

- **Add multiple check-ins for formative assessment:** These check-ins are built into the structure of the lesson. The check-ins meant that Mr. Collins didn't have to remember to check in with the students. Instead, the students came to him.

- **Establish a clear goal:** Mr. Collins established a clear goal that he shared with the students, as discussed in chapter 5 (page 73).

- **Use student self-reporting:** Mr. Collins used student self-reporting to evaluate the students. Research shows students are accurate when reporting their progress and abilities (Dueck, 2021). Mr. Collins provided the students with prompts to help guide the discussion; you can share prompts with students at the beginning of an activity.

What You Can Do Now

This book focuses on the *why* and the *how* of STEM education. This chapter focused on actual teaching techniques, told through grade-level vignettes. Let's talk about how you can get started with STEM education.

Establish a STEM Vision

Hopefully, you are now enthusiastic about teaching STEM. Next, you need a vision that helps guide everyone involved. The vision for your STEM implementation is the reason you are implementing STEM.

To choose a vision, ask yourself why you are excited to implement STEM, why you care about STEM, and what positive changes will happen because of STEM implementation. Don't confuse the tools or curriculum that you'll be using to teach STEM with the STEM vision. Your STEM vision is the why, and the curriculum or tools are the how.

Your STEM vision will then help you determine your strategy. For example, if your STEM vision is to increase all students' engagement by having them solve real-world STEM challenges, then you should adopt STEM into the core curriculum—that is the only way you are going to reach all students.

Share Your STEM Vision

You now have an amazing STEM vision for your school. Your next step is to share that vision. Sharing your STEM vision will create alignment with your administrators and any other teachers you may work with. Sharing the STEM vision will also make it easy to collaborate with those same people.

To effectively communicate your vision, keep it short. Keeping the STEM vision to a few sentences will make it easy to communicate. Another option is to create the STEM vision *with* your other stakeholders. This shared ownership can help create buy-in for everyone.

Create an Implementation Plan

Now that there is a shared vision, you can create the implementation details. Many people make the mistake of skipping directly to this step. As discussed earlier, the shared STEM vision sets the purpose of the implementation and then creates alignment. If everyone understands the goal, then they can feel empowered to be innovative in their attempts to achieve the goal. The insights shared in this book provide you with ideas and inspiration for how to approach integrated STEM learning, principles, and pedagogy.

EPILOGUE

In May 2022, I was at the VEX Robotics World Championship in Dallas, Texas, which was the first in-person Worlds in two years because of the COVID-19 pandemic. VEX Worlds began during Teacher Appreciation Week, and that fact resonated with me my entire time in Dallas. I heard from parents about how their children worked for hours on their robots. One parent shared the story of how his son left his phone in the car and didn't notice for days because he was so engrossed in coding his robot.

Students told me how much they loved solving problems and working with their team. They explained to me all the different iterations for their robot and their code. I never once heard the word *failure*.

A principal told me how his school's robotics program had energized his entire district. He explained how students were bonding over STEM and the authentic engagement they had with educational robotics.

Words, gestures, and gifts are all appropriate for Teacher Appreciation Week, but if we really appreciate teachers, then we'll take the excitement, passion, and engagement of competitive robotics and put them in every classroom. And how we can do that is by implementing STEM.

In chapter 5 (page 73), we discussed how memory is the residue of thought, but students will only think about the things they care about. The students at robotics competitions care because they can see how their work links to the world around them. STEM is a mirror to our world—finding cures for viruses, launching telescopes into space, and taking pictures of black holes are all examples of integrated STEM.

I loved teaching STEM and I love seeing students from all over the world engaged in STEM learning. I love STEM not because I am an engineer. When I have free time, I do not spend it coding or tinkering. I love STEM because it connects with the reason I became an educator: seeing students enthusiastic about and engaged with their learning. STEM brought my classroom to life, and it reignited my passion for teaching.

STEM can do the same for you and your students.

REFERENCES AND RESOURCES

Aijaz, A. (2019, February 11). *Release frequency: A need for speed*. Accessed at https://dzone .com/articles/release-frequency-a-need-for-speed on February 28, 2022.

Anderson, R. C., Graham, M., Kennedy, P., Nelson, N., Stoolmiller, M., Baker, S. K., & Fien, H. (2019). Student agency at the crux: Mitigating disengagement in middle and high school. *Contemporary Educational Psychology, 56*, 205–217. https://doi.org /10.1016/j.cedpsych.2018.12.005

Arnold, C. (2020, July 15). How computational immunology changed the face of COVID-19 vaccine development. *Nature Medicine*. Accessed at www.nature.com /articles/d41591-020-00027-9 on July 15, 2020.

Ball, P. (2020, December 18). The lightning-fast quest for COVID vaccines—and what it means for other diseases. *Nature*. Accessed at www.nature.com/articles/d41586-020 -03626-1 on July 26, 2022.

Beaty, A. (2007). *Iggy Peck, architect*. New York: Abrams Books for Young Readers.

Beaty, A. (2013). *Rosie Revere, engineer*. New York: Abrams Books for Young Readers.

Beaty, A. (2016). *Ada Twist, scientist*. New York: Abrams Books for Young Readers.

Becker, H. (2018). *Counting on Katherine: How Katherine Johnson saved Apollo 13*. New York: Henry Holt and Company.

Beghetto, R. A. (2016). Creative learning: A fresh look. *Journal of Cognitive Education and Psychology, 15*(1), 6–23. https://doi.org/10.1891/1945-8959.15.1.6

Beghetto, R. A. (2018). *What if? Building students' problem-solving skills through complex challenges*. Alexandria, VA: ASCD.

Beghetto, R. A., Kaufman, J. C., & Baer, J. (2015). *Teaching for creativity in the Common Core classroom*. New York: Teachers College Press, Columbia University.

Börnert-Ringleb, M., & Wilbert, J. (2018). The association of strategy use and concrete-operational thinking in primary school. *Frontiers in Education, 3.* https://doi.org/10.3389/feduc.2018.00038

Calderon, V. J., & Yu, D. (2017, June 1). Student enthusiasm falls as high school graduation nears. *Gallup News.* Accessed at https://news.gallup.com/opinion/gallup/211631/student-enthusiasm-falls-high-school-graduation-nears.aspx on June 1, 2022.

Cameron, C. E. (2018). *Hands on, minds on: How executive function, motor, and spatial skills foster school readiness.* New York: Teachers College Press.

Christensen, C. M. (2016). *The innovator's dilemma: When new technologies cause great firms to fail.* Boston: Harvard Business Review Press.

Citro, A. (2017). *Zoey and Sassafras: Dragons and marshmallows.* Woodinville, WA: Innovation Press.

Cooper, D. (with Catania, J.). (2022). *Rebooting assessment: A practical guide for balancing conversations, performances, and products.* Bloomington, IN: Solution Tree Press.

Costa, A. L., & Kallick, B. (Eds.). (2008). *Learning and leading with habits of mind: 16 essential characteristics for success.* Alexandria, VA: ASCD.

Davis, M. R. (2018, November 12). Raising student "voice and choice" is the mantra. But is it a good idea? *Education Week.* Accessed at www.edweek.org/technology/raising-student-voice-and-choice-is-the-mantra-but-is-it-a-good-idea/2018/11 on June 1, 2022.

Deisseroth, K. (2021). *Projections: A story of human emotions.* New York: Random House.

Derting, K., & Johannes, S. R. (2020). *Cece loves science.* New York: Greenwillow Books.

DiBenedetto, M. K., & Schunk, D. H. (2022). Assessing academic self-efficacy. In *M. S. Khine & T. Nielson (Eds.), Academic self-efficacy in education* (pp. 11–37). Springer. https://doi.org/10.1007/978-981-16-8240-7_2

DK. (2017). *Human body!* New York: DK.

Doidge, N. (2007). *The brain that changes itself: Stories of personal triumph from the frontiers of brain science.* New York: Penguin.

Dolgin, E. (2021, November 8). How protein-based COVID vaccines could change the pandemic. *Nature.* Accessed at www.nature.com/articles/d41586-021-03025-0 on November 11, 2021.

Donovan, J. (2019). *Shoot for the moon: The space race and the extraordinary voyage of Apollo 11*. New York: Little, Brown.

Dueck, M. (2014). *Grading smarter, not harder: Assessment strategies that motivate kids and help them learn*. Alexandria, VA: ASCD.

Dueck, M. (2021). *Giving students a say: Smarter assessment practices to empower and engage*. Alexandria, VA: ASCD.

DuFour, R., DuFour, R., Eaker, R., Many, T. W., & Mattos, M. (2016). *Learning by doing: A handbook for Professional Learning Communities at Work* (3rd ed.). Bloomington, IN: Solution Tree Press.

Dweck, C. S. (2017). *Mindset: The new psychology of success* (Updated ed.). New York: Ballantine Books.

Eason, S. H., & Levine, S. C. (2017, December 11). *Spatial reasoning: Why math talk is about more than numbers*. Stanford, CA: Development and Research in Early Math Education, Stanford University. Accessed at https://dreme.stanford.edu/news /spatial-reasoning-why-math-talk-about-more-numbers on August 15, 2022.

Ericsson, A., & Pool, R. (2016). *Peak: Secrets from the new science of expertise*. Boston: Houghton Mifflin Harcourt.

Feldman, J. (2019). *Grading for equity: What it is, why it matters, and how it can transform schools and classrooms*. Thousand Oaks, CA: Corwin.

Gibbons, G. (2018). *Galaxies, galaxies!* (Updated ed.). New York: Holiday House.

Guarino, B., Cha, A. E., Wood, J., & Witte, G. (2020, December 14). "The weapon that will end the war": First coronavirus vaccine shots given outside trials in U.S. *The Washington Post*. Accessed at https://washingtonpost.com/nation/2020/12/14/first -covid-vaccines-new-york on June 1, 2022.

Guzdial, M. (2016). *Learner-centered design of computing education: Research on computing for everyone*. San Rafael, CA: Morgan & Claypool.

Guzdial, M. (2020a, July 13). *Changing computer science education to eliminate structural inequities and in response to a pandemic: Starting a four part series* [Blog post]. Accessed at https://computinged.wordpress.com/2020/07/13/changing-computer -science-education-to-eliminate-structural-inequities-and-in-response-to-a-pandemic on August 14, 2022.

Guzdial, M. (2020b, July 27). *Proposal #2 to change CS education to reduce inequity: Make the highest grades achievable by all students* [Blog post]. Accessed at https://computinged.wordpress.com/2020/07/27/proposal-2-to-change-cs-education-to-reduce-inequity-stop-allocating-rationing-or-curving-down-grades on August 14, 2022.

Hattie, J., & Yates, G. (2014). *Visible learning and the science of how we learn.* New York: Routledge.

Hirsch, E. D., Jr. (1999). *The schools we need: And why we don't have them.* New York: Anchor Books.

Institute of Medicine & National Research Council. (2015). *Transforming the workforce for children birth through age 8: A unifying foundation.* Washington, DC: National Academies Press.

Kaufman, J. C., & Sternberg, R. J. (Eds.). (2019). *The Cambridge handbook of creativity* (2nd ed.). New York: Cambridge University Press.

Kaufman, P. (Director). (1983). *The right stuff* [Film]. United States: Ladd Company.

Kirschner, P. A., & Hendrick, C. (2020). *How learning happens: Seminal works in educational psychology and what they mean in practice.* New York: Routledge.

Kise, J. A. G. (2021). *Doable differentiation: Twelve strategies to meet the needs of all learners.* Bloomington, IN: Solution Tree Press.

Klein, T. (2020, May 21). *Grades fail at motivating students. Intrinsic motivation works better.* Accessed at https://edsurge.com/news/2020-05-21-grades-fail-at-motivating-students-intrinsic-motivation-works-better on June 1, 2022.

Kramer, J. (2020, December 31). They spent 12 years solving a scientific puzzle. It yielded the first COVID-19 vaccines. *National Geographic.* Accessed at https://nationalgeographic.com/science/article/these-scientists-spent-twelve-years-solving-puzzle-yielded-coronavirus-vaccines on June 1, 2022.

Kwon, D. (2019, March 18). Biologists discover unknown powers in mighty mitochondria. *Quanta Magazine.* Accessed at https://quantamagazine.org/shape-shifting-mitochondria-direct-stem-cells-fate-20190318 on June 1, 2022.

LaFee, S. (2021, March 18). *Novel coronavirus circulated undetected months before first COVID-19 cases in Wuhan, China.* UC San Diego Health News. Accessed at https://health.ucsd.edu/news/releases/Pages/2021-03-18-novel-coronavirus-circulated-undetected-months-before-first-covid-19-cases-in-wuhan-china.aspx on August 15, 2022.

Landhuis, E. (2021, November 2). Her machine learning tools pull insights from cell images. *Quanta Magazine*. Accessed at https://quantamagazine.org/anne-carpenters-ai-tools -pull-insights-from-cell-images-20211102 on June 1, 2022.

Lehrer, R., & Schauble, L. (2021). Stepping carefully: Thinking through the potential pitfalls of integrated STEM. *Journal for STEM Education Research*, *4*(1), 1–26. https://doi.org/10.1007/s41979-020-00042-y

Lemov, D. (2021). *Teach like a champion 3.0: 63 techniques that put students on the path to college.* Hoboken, NJ: Jossey-Bass.

Levy, F., & Murnane, R. (2013). *Dancing with robots: Human skills for computerized work.* Washington, DC: Third Way. Accessed at www.thirdway.org/report/dancing-with -robots-human-skills-for-computerized-work on August 25, 2022.

Lieberman, D. Z., & Long, M. E. (2018). *The molecule of more: How a single chemical in your brain drives love, sex, and creativity—and will determine the fate of the human race.* Dallas, TX: BenBella Books.

Livio, M. (2013, June 27). Brilliant blunders: How the big bang beat out the steady state universe. *NOVA.* Accessed at www.pbs.org/wgbh/nova/article/brilliant-blunders on August 15, 2022.

Lucido, A. (2019). *Emmy in the key of code.* Boston: Houghton Mifflin Harcourt.

Maguire, E. A., Woollett, K., & Spiers, H. J. (2006). London taxi drivers and bus drivers: A structural MRI and neuropsychological analysis. *Hippocampus*, *16*(12), 1091–1101. https://doi.org/10.1002/hipo.20233

Marshall, A. (2018). *Gary and the great inventors: It's laundry day!* Wilmington, DE: Our Children's Network.

Mayer, R. E. (2004). Should there be a three-strikes rule against pure discovery learning? *American Psychologist*, *59*(1), 14–19. https://doi.org/10.1037/0003-066x.59.1.14

McClure, E. R., Guernsey, L., Clements, D. H., Bales, S. N., Nichols, J., Kendall-Taylor, N., et al. (2017). *STEM starts early: Grounding science, technology, engineering, and math education in early childhood.* New York: The Joan Ganz Cooney Center at Sesame Workshop. Accessed at https://joanganzcooneycenter.org/wp-content /uploads/2017/01/jgcc_stemstartsearly_final.pdf on June 1, 2022.

Mccrea, P. (2020). *Motivated teaching: Harnessing the science of motivation to boost attention and effort in the classroom.* Scotts Valley, CA: CreateSpace.

Meltzer, B. (2014). *I am Amelia Earhart.* New York: Dial Books for Young Readers.

Meltzer, B. (2018). *I am Neil Armstrong.* New York: Dial Books for Young Readers.

Merrill, S., & Gonser, S. (2021, September 16). *The importance of student choice across all grade levels.* Edutopia. Accessed at https://edutopia.org/article/importance-student -choice-across-all-grade-levels on December 1, 2021.

Mosca, J. F. (2020). *The girl with a mind for math: The story of Raye Montague.* Woodinville, WA: Innovation Press.

Moss, J., Bruce, C. D., Caswell, B., Flynn, T., & Hawes, Z. (2016). *Taking shape: Activities to develop geometric and spatial thinking, grades K–2.* North York, Ontario, Canada: Pearson Canada.

NASA. (n.d.). *Mars 2020* Perseverance *rover.* Accessed at https://mars.nasa.gov/mars2020 on August 15, 2022.

NASA. (2022, July 12). *NASA's Webb sheds light on galaxy evolution, black holes.* Accessed at www.nasa.gov/image-feature/goddard/2022/nasa-s-webb-sheds-light -on-galaxy-evolution-black-holes on August 24, 2022.

National Academy of Engineering & National Research Council. (2014). *STEM integration in K–12 education: Status, prospects, and an agenda for research.* Washington, DC: National Academies Press.

National Research Council. (2012). *A framework for K–12 science education: Practices, crosscutting concepts, and core ideas.* Washington, DC: National Academies Press.

National Science Teaching Association. (2020, February). *STEM education teaching and learning* [Position statement]. Accessed at www.nsta.org/nstas-official-positions/ stem-education-teaching-and-learning on June 2, 2021.

Nayir, F. (2017). The relationship between student motivation and class engagement levels. *Eurasian Journal of Educational Research, 71,* 59–77. Accessed at https://files.eric.ed .gov/fulltext/EJ1158398.pdf on June 2, 2022.

NGSS Lead States. (2013a). *Appendix I: Engineering design in the NGSS.* Accessed at https://www.nextgenscience.org/sites/default/files/Appendix%20I%20-%20 Engineering%20Design%20in%20NGSS%20-%20FINAL_V2.pdf on August 30, 2022.

NGSS Lead States. (2013b). *Next Generation Science Standards: For states, by states.* Washington, DC: National Academies Press.

No Child Left Behind (NCLB) Act of 2001, Pub. L. No. 107-110, § 115, Stat. 1425 (2002).

O'Callaghan, J. (2022, May 12). Black hole image reveals the beast inside the Milky Way's heart. *Quanta Magazine*. Accessed at https://quantamagazine.org/black-hole-image -reveals-sagittarius-a-20220512 on August 24, 2022.

Pausch, R. (2008). *The last lecture*. New York: Hyperion.

Pavlus, J. (2019, July 24). His artificial intelligence sees inside living cells. *Quanta Magazine*. Accessed at https://quantamagazine.org/greg-johnsons-artificial -intelligence-sees-inside-living-cells-20190724 on June 2, 2022.

Peckham, O. (2021, March 11). *Behind the Gordon Bell Prize–winning spike protein simulations*. HPCwire. Accessed at https://hpcwire.com/2021/03/11/behind-the -gordon-bell-prize-winning-spike-protein-simulations on June 2, 2022.

Puntambekar, S., & Hubscher, R. (2010). Tools for scaffolding students in a complex learning environment: What have we gained and what have we missed? *Educational Psychologist, 40*(1), 1–12. https://doi.org/10.1207/s15326985ep4001_1

Resnick, M. (2017). *Lifelong kindergarten: Cultivating creativity through projects, passion, peers, and play*. Cambridge, MA: MIT Press.

Reuell, P. (2019, April 10). A black hole, revealed. *The Harvard Gazette*. Accessed at https://news.harvard.edu/gazette/story/2019/04/harvard-scientists-shed-light-on -importance-of-black-hole-image on August 15, 2022.

Ripley, D. (2022). *The tactical teacher: Proven strategies to positively influence student learning and classroom behavior*. Bloomington, IN: Solution Tree Press.

Sherrington, T. (2019). *The learning rainforest: Great teaching in real classrooms*. Blairsville, PA: Learning Sciences International.

Shu, C. (2019, April 10). *The creation of the algorithm that made the first black hole image possible was led by MIT grad student Katie Bouman*. Accessed at https://techcrunch .com/2019/04/10/the-creation-of-the-algorithm-that-made-the-first-black-hole -image-possible-was-led-by-mit-grad-student-katie-bouman on June 2, 2022.

Sullivan, A. A. (2019). *Breaking the STEM stereotype: Reaching girls in early childhood*. Lanham, MD: Rowman & Littlefield.

Unger, M., & Blake, A. V. (2021). *Capturing creativity: 20 easy ways to bring low-tech STEAM into your classroom*. Morrisville, NC: Lulu Press.

van Kesteren, M. T. R., Krabbendam, L., & Meeter, M. (2018). Integrating educational knowledge: Reactivation of prior knowledge during educational learning enhances memory integration. *npj Science of Learning, 3*(11). https://doi.org/10.1038/s41539 -018-0027-8

VEX GO Labs. (n.d.a). *Intro to building: Unit letter home.* Accessed at https://education .vex.com/stemlabs/go/intro-to-building/unit-overview/letter-home on August 24, 2022.

VEX GO Labs. (n.d.b). *Mars rover-surface operations.* Accessed at https://education.vex .com/stemlabs/go/mars-rover-surface-operations on August 24, 2022.

VEX IQ. (n.d.). *STEM lab letters home & checklists.* Accessed at https://kb.vex.com/hc /en-us/articles/360060822531-VEX-IQ-STEM-Lab-Letters-Home-Checklists on August 24, 2022.

Wall, M. (2015, November 4). *NASA to unveil new findings about Mars' atmosphere Thursday.* Yahoo! News. Accessed at www.yahoo.com/news/weather/nasa-unveil -findings-mars-atmosphere-thursday-230201135.html on August 16, 2022.

Wechsler, D. (2017). *The hidden life of a toad.* Watertown, MA: Charlesbridge.

Weintrop, D., Beheshti, E., Horn, M., Orton, K., Jona, K., Trouille, L., et al. (2016). Defining computational thinking for mathematics and science classrooms. *Journal of Science Education and Technology, 25*(1), 127–147. https://doi.org/10.1007 /s10956-015-9581-5

Whiting, K. (2020, October 21). *These are the top 10 job skills of tomorrow—and how long it takes to learn them.* World Economic Forum. Accessed at www.weforum.org/agenda /2020/10/top-10-work-skills-of-tomorrow-how-long-it-takes-to-learn-them on June 3, 2022.

Wiliam, D. (2018a). *Creating the schools our children need: Why what we're doing now won't help much (and what we can do instead).* Blairsville, PA: Learning Sciences International.

Wiliam, D. (2018b). *Embedded formative assessment* (2nd ed.). Bloomington, IN: Solution Tree Press.

Wiliam, D. (2020, April 6). *Teacher quality: What it is, why it matters, and how to get more of it* [Video file]. Accessed at https://youtube.com/watch?v=bE8Tp37pU54 on June 7, 2022.

Wiliam, D., Brookhart, S., Guskey, T., & McTighe, J. (2020). *Grading in a comprehensive and balanced assessment system* [Policy paper]. Blairsville, PA: Learning Sciences International.

Willingham, D. T. (2021a, April 13). *How to foster creativity in children.* Accessed at www.yahoo.com/video/foster-creativity-children-150914764.html on June 2, 2022.

Willingham, D. T. (2021b). *Why don't students like school? A cognitive scientist answers questions about how the mind works and what it means for the classroom* (2nd ed.). Hoboken, NJ: Jossey-Bass.

Winter, J. (2017). *The world is not a rectangle: A portrait of architect Zaha Hadid.* San Diego, CA: Beach Lane Books.

Witherspoon, E. B., Higashi, R. M., Schunn, C. D., Baehr, E. C., & Shoop, R. (2018). Developing computational thinking through a virtual robotics programming curriculum. *ACM Transactions on Computing Education, 18*(1), 1–20. https://doi .org/10.1145/3104982

Wolchover, N. (2021, December 3). The Webb space telescope will rewrite cosmic history. If it works. *Quanta Magazine.* Accessed at https://quantamagazine.org/why-nasas -james-webb-space-telescope-matters-so-much-20211203 on August 24, 2022.

World Economic Forum. (2020). *The future of jobs report 2020.* Cologny, Switzerland: Author. Accessed at www.weforum.org/reports/the-future-of-jobs-report-2020 on August 24, 2022.

Zuckerman, G. (2021). *A shot to save the world: The inside story of the life-or-death race for a COVID-19 vaccine.* New York: Portfolio/Penguin.

Zuckerman, G., & Loftus, P. (2021, February 23). Novavax nears COVID-19 vaccine game changer—after years of failure. *The Wall Street Journal.* Accessed at www .wsj.com/articles/novavax-nears-covid-19-vaccine-game-changerafter-years-of -failure-11614096579 on June 2, 2022.

INDEX

D

Dancing with Robots: Human Skills for Computerized Work (Levy and Murnane), 95

deBruyn, J., 66–69

Deisseroth, K., 104–105

designing and creating a chair or bed for your favorite stuffed animal, 59–62

designing and creating a container for the egg drop challenge, 62–64

discussions
  classroom discussions, 80–82
  conversation-based grading and, 104–106
  current events discussions, 15
  guided discovery learning and, 80
  norms and, 41
  parent discussions, 15

divergent thinking, 126

Dueck, M., 96, 113–115

E

egg drop challenge, designing and creating a container for, 62–64

elevator pitches, 113–114

Embedded Formative Assessment (Wiliam), 96

engagement, choice, and collaboration
  about, 37
  classroom management and student motivation and, 46–47
  collaborating to enhance learning, 47–50
  key takeaways for, 54
  motivating students, 37–46

teacher spotlight: motivating students in a STEM classroom, 52–54
  what you can do now, 50–52

engagement, three dimensions of, 37, 38

engineering. *See also* STEM narratives
  definition of, 58
  exploring science and engineering, 8–9

engineering centers, 16

engineering design process (EDP)
  creativity and, 124–126
  embracing engineering design process, 65
  exploring science and engineering, 8
  failure and, 58–64
  formative assessment strategies and, 111
  steps of, 58
  vignette for organizing STEM learning while building a tower, 131–133

engineering notebooks
  examples for, 109, 110
  formative assessments and, 100, 102
  grading and, 106
  routines and, 40
  using an engineering notebook in grades K-3, 109–110
  vignette with, 97–98, 99, 140–141, 144

executive function, 22–24

exit tickets, 65, 111

exploring STEM and creativity. *See* creativity

exploring STEM teaching and guided discovery learning. *See* guided discovery learning

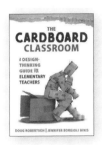

The Cardboard Classroom
By Doug Robertson with Jennifer Borgioli Binis

In *The Cardboard Classroom*, authors Doug Robertson and
Jennifer Borgioli Binis offer practical guidance and sample
projects developed from Robertson's authentic classroom
experiences to help you find space for this engaging approach
to instruction in your daily practice.

BKG023

Designing the Future
By Ann Kaiser

No matter the subject or grade, giving students engineering design
challenges encourages creativity, communication, innovation,
and collaboration. Throughout the book, you will find more than 25
easy-entry, low-risk engineering activities and projects you can
begin immediately incorporating into existing classwork.

BKF853

The New Art and Science of Teaching Science
By Brett Erdmann, Steven M. Wood, Troy Gobble, Robert J. Marzano

Strengthen science education practice based on Robert J. Marzano's
instructional framework, *The New Art and Science of Teaching*. Driven
by data, this book positions teachers to promote student learning
as they engage in strategies and activities to enhance teaching and
student achievement in science.

BKF808

The New Art and Science of Teaching Mathematics
By Nathan D. Lang-Raad and Robert J. Marzano

Discover how to make the most of the groundbreaking New Art and
Science of Teaching model in mathematics classrooms. Readers
will discover myriad strategies and tools for articulating learning
goals, conducting lessons, tracking students' progress, and more.

BKF810

Solution Tree | Press

a division of

Solution Tree

Visit SolutionTree.com or call 800.733.6786 to order.

Quality team learning **from authors you trust**

Global PD Teams is the first-ever **online professional development resource designed to support your entire faculty on your learning journey.** This convenient tool offers daily access to videos, mini-courses, eBooks, articles, and more packed with insights and research-backed strategies you can use immediately.

GET STARTED
SolutionTree.com/**GlobalPDTeams**
800.733.6786